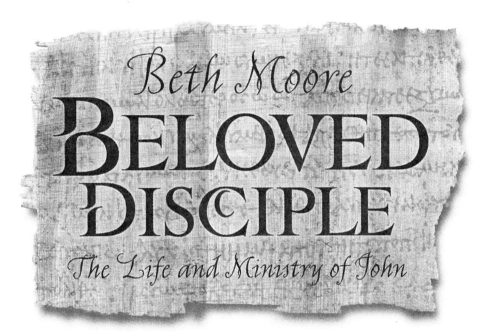

Beth Moore

BELOVED DISCIPLE

The Life and Ministry of John

LEADER GUIDE

Julie Woodruff

Retreat Plans by Cheris Gaston

LifeWay Press
Nashville, Tennessee

ISBN 0-6330-1853-8

Dewey Decimal Classification Number: 225.92
Subject Headings: JOHN, APOSTLE
BIBLE.N.T. JOHN—STUDY
DISCIPLESHIP TRAINING—WOMEN

Editor in Chief: Dale McCleskey
Art Director: Jon Rodda
Editors: Joyce McGregor and David Haney
Copy Editor: Beth Shive

Unless otherwise indicated, Scripture quotations are from the Holy Bible,
New International Version, copyright © 1973, 1978, 1984 by International Bible Society.

Scripture quotations identified KJV are from the *King James Version.*

Scripture quotations identified NASB are from the NEW AMERICAN STANDARD BIBLE,
© Copyright The Lockman Foundation, 1960, 1962, 1963, 1968, 1971, 1972, 1973, 1975, 1977, 1995.
Used by permission.

To order additional copies of this resource, write to LifeWay Church Resources Customer Service;
One LifeWay Plaza; Nashville, TN 37234-0013; fax (615) 251-5933;
phone toll free (800) 458-2772; email *customerservice@lifeway.com;* order online at *www.lifeway.com;*
or visit the LifeWay Christian Store serving you.

Printed in the United States of America

Leadership and Adult Publishing
LifeWay Church Resources
One LifeWay Plaza
Nashville, TN 37234-0175

Introduction

*B*eloved Disciple is an in-depth study of the life of John the apostle and his relationship with the One who loved him. The goal of our study is to get to know John's heart as Christ's beloved disciple and to let him lead us deeper into the depths of Christ's inexhaustible love. As we travel this journey with the beloved disciple, we will grow, as John did, in our desire to follow our Master and to love Him with all our being.

This guide has been prepared to equip you to plan and lead a study of *Beloved Disciple* for groups in your church or community. You will find administrative guidance, help for planning and promoting the study, and step-by-step instructions for conducting the group-study sessions.

COURSE OVERVIEW

This in-depth course was designed to be completed over 11 weeks through a combination of daily, individual study and weekly group sessions.

INDIVIDUAL STUDY

Each participant needs a copy of *Beloved Disciple* member book, which contains reading assignments and activities designed to reinforce and apply learning. The member book is divided into an introduction and 10 weeks of content. Every week's material contains 5 daily lessons, each requiring about 45 minutes to complete. Participants complete the daily reading and the learning activities at home in preparation for the weekly group sessions.

GROUP SESSIONS

Participants meet once each week for a two-hour group session that guides them to discuss and apply what they have learned during their daily, individual study. *Beloved Disciple* offers two options for conducting a group study. Choose the format that will best meet the needs of your group and that will best suit your skills as a facilitator.

Plan A. This format, best suited for groups with a large attendance, utilizes both large- and small-group learning experiences. The small-group portion of this session encourages accountability and allows members to benefit from the insights of other participants as they process the material they have studied during the week. The small groups also help build relationships as partic-

ipants share prayer concerns and pray together. In the large-group time each week, members watch video presentations in which Beth Moore enhances the material in the member book.

For members to receive the greatest possible benefit from plan A, schedule a 2-hour group session each week, plus a 15-minute check-in period. Following this procedure ensures that members receive the blessings of intimate experiences with God through daily study, support and fellowship through small-group discussions, and inspiration through the video presentations. The session-leadership suggestions labeled *Plan A* in this guide reflect the following schedule, although times shown here are arbitrary examples.

8:45 Child care open, attendance and homework check (15 mins.)

9:00 Large group—welcome, worship, and prayer (15 mins.)

9:15 Small groups (45 mins.)
 • Prayer (5 mins.)
 • Discussion of Principle Questions (20 mins.)
 • Discussion of Personal Discussion Questions (20 mins.)

10:00 Break and return to large group (5 mins.)

10:05 Large group (55 mins.)
 • Video presentation (50 mins.)
 • Closing assignment and prayer (5 mins.)

11:00 Dismiss

This schedule is ideal for a weekday or a weeknight study. It may also be followed for the church's Discipleship Training period if the study is begun an hour earlier and does not interfere with other church activities.

Some elements of this format may be adjusted to your preferences or needs. For example, you may prefer to add time for a longer break between the small- and large-group periods. Feel free to adjust the schedule, but we encourage you not to omit any one of the three key ingredients of this learning model:

1. Individual study of the member book at home
2. Small-group discussion of the Principle Questions and the Personal Discussion Questions in each week's material in the member book
3. Large-group viewing of the videos

Here is an overview of the procedures for each segment of the session for groups using plan A.

- Child care open, attendance and homework check (15 mins.). Allow time for mothers to leave children in child-care facilities before the session. Each participant must check in outside the large-group meeting room and have homework reviewed by the small-group facilitator. The facilitator does not check for correct responses but verifies that work is complete.
- Large group—welcome, worship, and prayer (15 mins.). The large-group leader is responsible for convening the group and conducting this portion of the session. You may wish to plan special music or select an appropriate hymn or praise song for the group to sing. End this segment with prayer for the day's learning experience.
- Small-group discussion (45 mins.). If the number of participants is small, remain in one group for this segment. If you enroll more than 12 people, however, plan for a small group for every 10 to 12 people and enlist a small-group facilitator for each group. These facilitators are responsible for taking prayer requests, having a prayer time (5 mins.), and guiding participants to discuss the Principle Questions (20 mins.) and Personal Discussion Questions (20 mins.) in each week's material in the member book.
- Return to large group (5 mins.). This transitional time allows time for a brief break. Provide light refreshments if desired.
- Video presentation (50 mins.). A video presentation by Beth Moore is provided in the leader kit for each week's group session. The large-group leader should play the appropriate video at this time. Participants complete the corresponding video response sheet at the end of each week's material in their member books as they view the video.
- Closing assignment and prayer (5 mins.). The large-group leader encourages participants to complete the next week's daily assignments and closes with a prayer of praise or thanksgiving.

Plan B. In this approach, instead of having large- and small-group learning periods, participants remain together for the entire group session. Instead of focusing on the Principle Questions and Personal Discussion Questions, the session plans provide a variety of activities that engage members in the content of the week's study. Designed primarily for smaller groups, this format allows more interaction and provides the leader more detailed suggestions for involving members in learning.

Of course, you may choose to follow plan A and select certain ideas or activities from plan B. Always pray and follow the Holy Spirit's leadership to determine the procedures that are best for your group.

Plan B follows these procedures.

- Child care open, attendance and homework check (15 mins.). Allow time for mothers to leave children in child-care facilities before the session. Each participant must check in outside the meeting room and have homework reviewed by the group leader. The leader does not check for correct responses but verifies that work is complete.
- Small-group discussion (55 mins.). These group leader is responsible for taking prayer requests, having a prayer time (5 mins.), and guiding participants through the procedures listed under *Plan B* in each session of this guide (50 mins.).
- Video presentation (50 mins.). A video presentation by Beth Moore is provided in the leader kit for each week's group session. The group leader should play the appropriate video at this time. Participants complete the corresponding video response sheet at the end of each week's material in their member books as they view the video.
- Closing assignment and prayer (5 mins.). The group leader encourages participants to complete the next week's daily assignments and closes with a prayer of praise or thanksgiving.

The session-leadership suggestions labeled *Plan B* in this guide reflect the following schedule, although times shown here are arbitrary examples.

8:45	Child care open, attendance and homework check (15 mins.)
9:00	Group session—welcome, prayer, and discussion (55 mins.)
9:55	Break (10 mins.)
10:05	Group session continues (55 mins.) • Video presentation (50 mins.) • Closing assignment and prayer (5 mins.)
11:00	Dismiss

Optional formats. A format of an introductory session plus 2 hours per week for 10 weeks is ideal for *Beloved Disciple;* however, you may need another option to fit your group's situation. Many groups study these materials with an alternative schedule. The problem with studying on a schedule other than one unit per week is that members do not get into the regular habit of daily Bible study.

If you adopt an alternative plan, please take steps to encourage members to study the Bible daily. If your group can meet for only one hour per week, consider viewing the video one week and conducting the group study the next. To maintain the continuity of daily study, encourage members to complete the daily work in the member book during the first week. Then encourage them to review the work daily during the second week. Ask them to write down their answers to the Principle Questions and Personal Discussion Questions each day during their review.

Some groups meet once a month. If your group meets on some schedule other than weekly or biweekly, consider using an aid to encourage daily Bible study. One such resource is called *Day by Day in God's Kingdom* (item 0-7673-2577-X). It is a discipleship journal built around six Christian disciplines. It allows disciples to record their spiritual journeys as they study courses such as *Beloved Disciple*. Another journal members can use is *Whispers of Hope* by Beth Moore (item 0-7673-9278-7). Ask your members to complete the work in *Beloved Disciple* during the first week of the month and to review the material the week before the group meets.

RESOURCES

These resources are available for leaders and participants.

- *Beloved Disciple* (member book) provides an introduction and 10 weeks of daily, biblical studies on the life of John. The book also includes response sheets for video presentations. Each participant needs a copy of the member book. Order item 0-6330-1851-1.
- *Beloved Disciple Leader Kit* contains one copy of the member book, this leader guide, and six videotapes. Five of the videotapes (tapes 2–6) feature 10 lectures in which Beth Moore teaches material related to the content of the book. These segments were taped on location in Greece. The sixth video (tape 1) provides content for an introductory group session, two brief promotional segments that include a 30-second spot for use on local television stations, and a music video. (These videos are not available separately.) Order item 0-6330-1852-X.
- *Beloved Disciple Leader Guide* (the guide you are now reading) offers step-by-step directions for facilitating 11 group sessions, using *Beloved Disciple* and the videotapes included in the leader kit. This guide, one copy of which is included in the leader kit, is available separately. Order item number 0-6330-1853-8.
- *Beloved Disciple Audio CD Collection* includes the audio portions of Beth Moore's video presentations on 11 audio CDs, with a 16-page listening guide.

Although the CDs were designed for individual study, a leader may wish to use them for personal review and inspiration. Order item 0-6330-1854-6.
- *Worship Collection CD* (item 0-6330-2294-2) and *Cassette* (item 0-6330-2295-0) feature worship and praise music arranged and produced by Travis Cottrell. These are ideal selections for opening, closing, and transitional times in the group or for the worship portions of plan A.

You will also need the following materials.
- Registration tables
- Small signs that indicate divisions of the alphabet—A–E, F–J, K–O, P–S, T–Z, for example (plan A).
- Registration cards
- An attendance sheet for each small-group facilitator (plan A)
- Name tags and pencils
- Bibles
- A videotape player and monitor

PLAN A—LARGE & SMALL GROUPS

LEADERSHIP RESPONSIBILITIES

The following are descriptions of the roles and responsibilities of leaders for groups using plan A.

Large-group leader. This leader is not a teacher but an organizer, coordinator, and facilitator. The large-group leader's responsibilities include—
- providing administrative leadership for the group;
- scheduling the study;
- promoting the study and coordinating enrollment efforts;
- enlisting and coordinating the work of small-group facilitators;
- ordering and distributing resources;
- maintaining and submitting accurate records of participation each week as Discipleship Training attendance;
- leading the large-group segments of the weekly group sessions.

The large-group leader should be someone who is interested in exploring the crucial truths of this course and who desires to help others grow in intimacy with God. A long list of qualifications and years of teaching experience are not required. A heart prepared by God—being available and teachable—is more important. Paramount to this leader's success is a strong commitment to the study of this course and a faithful fulfillment of the basic responsibilities of group leadership.

This leader guide provides the large-group leader

administrative help for organizing a Bible-study group. It also gives specific guidance to prepare for and lead 11 group sessions.

Small-group facilitators. Enlist a small-group facilitator for every 10 to 12 participants. Again, these are not teachers but facilitators of the small groups' discussion and fellowship. Their responsibilities include—

- greeting and registering participants at the introductory session;
- calling members assigned to their small groups after the introductory session to introduce themselves, to tell them the locations of their small-group meeting rooms, and to encourage them to complete the daily assignments in week 1 of the member book;
- checking small-group members' attendance and homework prior to each week's meeting;
- taking prayer requests, conducting a prayer time at the beginning of the small-group period, praying for participants, and encouraging participants to pray for one another;
- guiding members to discuss the Principle Questions (listed at the beginning of each week's material in the member book) and the Personal Discussion Questions (designated by the hand symbol ✍ in the member book);
- promoting fellowship among group members;
- noting opportunities for follow-up ministry.

If you have 12 or fewer participants, one leader can serve both the large- and small-group function when following plan A. Each session of this guide designates the point during the session when small-group discussion is to occur. Share with each small-group facilitator a list of responsibilities and the following information about facilitating and handling problems in small groups.

FACILITATING DISCUSSION

You will find many applications in this study for a contemporary walk with God. Beth Moore applies many of the course's concepts in her video presentations. In addition, the member book encourages participants to apply what they are learning as they complete their daily assignments.

One purpose of the small-group discussion period each week is to enable members to make meaningful application to their daily lives. Small-group facilitators will guide discussions of each week's Principle Questions, listed at the beginning of each week's material in the member book, as well as the Personal Discussion Questions. Small-group facilitators can use the following guidelines to make these discussion times effective in challenging participants spiritually and in promoting life change.

- Arrange the chairs in the meeting room in a circle or a semicircle so that participants can see one another. Seating should not physically exclude anyone.
- Greet members as they arrive. Start the meeting on time. Allow 5 minutes for prayer requests; then pray or ask a participant to pray. Make notes when requests are shared. Assure members that you are concerned not only about their spiritual growth but also about their personal lives. Encourage them to pray for one another during the week. If someone is experiencing difficult circumstances, write a note or call between sessions to say that you are praying.
- Spend 20 minutes discussing the week's Principle Questions (listed at the beginning of the week's material in the member book) and 20 minutes discussing Personal Discussion Questions (designated by the symbol ✍ in the member book). Emphasize that only participants who wish to respond should do so; no one is required to share responses. Do not force the discussion questions on members. Adapt and change them as necessary. Be flexible if members wish to spend more time on one group of questions or if they raise specific issues. Be sensitive to members' particular needs as the discussion progresses. Remember that your job is not to teach the material but to encourage and lead participants in sharing their insights about the work they have done during the week and in applying the content to their spiritual journeys.
- Be personally involved without relinquishing leadership. A facilitator's role is that of a fellow disciple who shares the same struggles the other participants have in their spiritual lives. You need to be emotionally vulnerable and willing to share your own feelings and responses. However, recognize that someone must lead the group and direct the discussion at all times. Be flexible, but do not allow the discussion to veer off on a tangent. Keep the focus on the week's content and its application.
- Try to create a relaxed atmosphere that will help every member feel a sense of belonging. Use first names. Do not rush the discussion.
- Pray for the Holy Spirit's leadership; then allow Him freedom to direct the session as He wills. His movement may be evident in tears of joy or conviction, emotional or spiritual brokenness, or the thrill of a newfound insight. Be sensitive to signs of God's work in a person's life and follow up by asking the person to share. Giving participants the opportunity to testify to what God is doing is very important. Often,

the testimony may help another person with a similar issue. Follow the Holy Spirit's leadership as God works in these discussion times.

• Be sure that you do not talk too much as facilitator. Do not be afraid of periods of silence.

• Be an encourager. Show a caring, loving spirit. Communicate acceptance and concern, especially if your group includes non-Christians. Create an atmosphere that communicates, "I accept you as you are." Accepting participants does not necessarily mean that you agree with their values or choices. You can love a person without agreeing with her. If a participant shares something that makes her feel vulnerable or ashamed, say something like: "I know your sharing took a lot of courage. I admire you for being willing to share it."

• Listen intently and aggressively. When someone shares something personal or painful, lean toward her. Use facial expressions to show concern. Nod your head.

• Be ready to address special needs that members may reveal. If someone is unsaved, follow the Holy Spirit's leadership to know the right time to talk with the person privately to lead her to Christ. If a participant reveals emotional pain or family problems, assure her of the group's concern and support and pause briefly to pray with the person. Then offer to meet with her later to help her find additional help if needed.

• Set boundaries. Do not permit a group member to act in a verbally abusive way toward another member. Do not force group members to do or say anything they are not willing to do or say. Try gently nudging a group member to a point of discovery and growth instead of pushing her to a conclusion for which she is not ready.

• Be enthusiastic!

• End the discussion period on time. You will face a challenge each week in bringing the discussion to an end in time for members to have a five-minute break before the large group reconvenes. At the first session emphasize the need to conclude on time each week. A few minutes before time to end the discussion period, help the person speaking reach a point of closure. Ask if anyone has anything to add. Allow response; then at some point end the discussion. If someone is not finished, affirm the importance of what the person is saying. Offer to continue the discussion next week and ask that member to introduce the topic at the beginning of the next meeting. Or you may need to spend time privately with the person if the topic does not relate to the entire group. Be sure you have tied loose ends. Did you put someone on hold during the discussion? Did you get back to the person? Was someone's sharing interrupted as you moved to focus on someone else's response? Did you reach closure with the original speaker? Finally, remind group members to pray for one another during the week.

COPING WITH PROBLEMS

No matter how meaningful the study and how effective the leadership, difficulties can arise. Following are common problems and suggestions for dealing with them.

Absenteeism. Absentees miss a potentially life-changing experience and diminish others' learning. If a participant is absent, contact the person, communicate your concern, and encourage her to make up the work. Otherwise, a participant will quickly get further behind and will likely drop out.

Not completing at-home assignments. Emphasize in the introductory session that a significant course requirement is doing daily study at home, including completion of the learning activities. State that each person's book will be checked before each session to see that homework was completed. Anyone unwilling to make this commitment should not participate in the study.

If someone has not completed the week's assignments, encourage the person to stay up-to-date to gain the greatest benefits from the study. If someone continually refuses to complete the assignments, meet with her and suggest that she withdraw and participate at a time when she can devote herself adequately to the study.

Disagreement with the content. Some debate in a group is productive. Remember that the Scriptures should always be the final source of authority. If debate becomes counterproductive, suggest that you and the participant discuss the matter later so that other members can participate in the present discussion.

Do not feel threatened if someone expects you to be an authority and to answer all of her questions. Emphasize your role as the facilitator of the discussion, pointing out that participants are to learn from one another and that you are not an authority on the subject. Suggest that a volunteer research the question during the week and report at the next meeting if the person insists that an answer is important to her.

A participant who dominates the group. Ways a person may dominate a group are—

• claiming a major portion of each discussion period to talk about her issues;

- repeatedly waiting until the last 10 minutes to introduce an emotionally charged story or problem;
- attempting to block other group members' sharing;
- judging others' behavior or confessions;
- challenging your leadership in a hostile way;
- criticizing other group members' motives or feelings.

As the facilitator, make sure every person has an opportunity to share. Discourage dominating members by calling on others, by asking someone to speak who has not yet responded, or by focusing directly on someone else. If these methods do not work, talk privately with the dominating person and enlist the person's support in involving everyone in future discussions.

When a person is going into too much detail and is losing the attention of the group, you will usually notice that the group has disconnected. Direct the sharing back on course by discreetly interrupting the person and by restating the point she is trying to make: "So what you are saying is …" Another method is to interrupt and restate the question you originally asked: "And Liz, what did you learn about God's love through that experience?" Even if the speaker is unsettled by this response, she should respond by restating the response more succinctly.

PLAN B—SMALL GROUP ONLY

LEADERSHIP RESPONSIBILITIES
Leaders in groups using plan B need to be responsible for—
- providing administrative leadership for the group;
- scheduling the study;
- promoting the study and coordinating enrollment;
- ordering and distributing resources;
- maintaining and submitting records of participation each week as Discipleship Training attendance;
- greeting and registering participants at the introductory session;
- checking members' attendance and homework prior to each week's meeting;
- taking prayer requests, conducting a prayer time at the beginning of the session, praying for participants, and encouraging participants to pray for one another;
- facilitating each group study session, following the suggestions provided under *Plan B* in each session of this guide;
- communicating with members periodically to offer help and to encourage them to complete their daily assignments in the member book;
- promoting fellowship among group members;
- noting opportunities for follow-up ministry.

You would benefit from reading the previous sections, "Facilitating Discussion" and "Coping with Problems." Although you can ignore the references to the Principle Questions and the Personal Discussion Questions, you can easily adapt the other suggestions to your responsibilities as a leader of a group that is following plan B.

PLANNING STEPS

The following steps are suggested to assist a group leader in organizing a study of *Beloved Disciple*.
1. Enlist the support of your pastor. His endorsement will encourage women to deepen their spiritual lives. Perhaps he will agree to announce from the pulpit this discipleship opportunity.
2. Talk with the likely participants to determine the level of interest in this type of in-depth study. Ask whether the study should be offered during the day, in the evening, or both. When scheduling the study, be sensitive to the needs of women who work outside the home.
3. Schedule 11 weeks on the church calendar that will allow the greatest participation. Fall and spring studies usually result in more participation than summer sessions do. However, summertime may afford some persons with seasonal careers—such as schoolteachers—an opportunity to attend.
4. Offer child care if possible. This will increase your attendance and ensure greater weekly participation.
5. Allow two hours for each weekly session. This time period will allow ample opportunities for both weekly activities: discussion of participants' home study and viewing of the week's video presentation.
6. After estimating the number of participants, order member books (item 0-6330-1851-1) four to six weeks in advance. Write to LifeWay Church Resources Customer Service; One LifeWay Plaza; Nashville, TN 37234-0113; fax order to (615) 251-5933; phone (800) 458-2772; email to *customerservice@lifeway.com;* order online at *www.lifeway.com;* or visit the LifeWay Christian Store serving you. Decide whether the church will pay for member books or whether participants will pay for their own. Experience has shown that if members pay for their books or a portion of the cost, they are likely to make a more serious commitment to the study. You may want to provide scholarships for members who cannot afford to purchase books.
7. If you are using plan A, find a meeting room that will accommodate your large-group sessions and reserve it for the duration of the study. Reserve small-group

meeting rooms for the number of groups you will have. Arrange the meeting rooms to be as intimate as possible. Chairs in the small-group rooms should be arranged in circles or semicircles. Semicircular rows of chairs are acceptable for the large-group room as long as all participants can view the video.

8. If you are using plan A, conduct a planning session for the large-group leader and the small-group facilitators. Complete the following actions in the meeting.

- Obtain copies of this leader guide for your small-group facilitators. Discuss the group-session format and their responsibilities, which include:
  —greeting and registering participants at the introductory session;
  —calling members assigned to their small groups after the introductory session to introduce themselves, explain the locations of their small-group meeting rooms, and encourage them to complete the daily assignments for week 1;
  —checking small-group members' attendance and homework prior to each week's meeting;
  —taking prayer requests, conducting a prayer time at the beginning of the small-group period, praying for participants, and encouraging participants to pray for one another;
  —guiding members to discuss the Principle Questions (listed at the beginning of each week's material in the member book) and the Personal Discussion Questions;
  —promoting fellowship among group members;
  —noting opportunities for follow-up ministry.

- Discuss registration procedures. Plan on setting up several registration tables outside the large-group meeting room with signs indicating divisions of the alphabet. For example, participants whose last names begin with A–E will register at one station, F–J at the next, K–O at the next, P–S at the next, and T–Z at the final station. Assign small-group facilitators to handle registration at the stations. The members registered by a particular facilitator would become members of her group. Make adjustments if numbers fall unevenly. Instruct the facilitators to be at their stations 30 minutes before registration begins at the introductory session. Provide them with a supply of member books, registration cards, pencils, and reusable name tags. Tell each registrar that she has the responsibility of making a good first impression. She needs to wear a name tag, greet members with enthusiasm, answer their questions as best she can or promise to find out the answers, make them feel welcome, and direct them to the large-group session. At subsequent sessions the small-group facilitators will follow the same procedures to check attendance and homework.

- Explain that after the introductory session small-group facilitators will transfer names from their registration cards to attendance sheets that you will provide. Each week they will record attendance, completion of homework, and prayer requests on this sheet. Emphasize that facilitators are merely to check whether participants have responded to the learning activities in the member book, not to determine whether responses are correct.

9. Promote the study, using the suggestions provided in the following section.

10. Plan to keep accurate records and report attendance to the church office. Regardless of when the study is offered, it is a Discipleship Training study and should be reported as Discipleship Training participation on the Annual Church Profile. Another reason to keep accurate participation records is that participants can earn Christian Growth Study Plan diplomas for completing the study. For details see the requirements on page 224 of the member book.

11. Pray, pray, and keep praying that God will involve the members He desires and that He will validate this study with His obvious presence and activity!

PROMOTING THE STUDY

This study provides a wonderful opportunity for outreach because it is free of rules and does not require a particular church affiliation. Target persons in your community who are interested in Bible study. Church bulletins, newsletters, handouts, posters, fliers at Mothers' Day Out, announcements in worship services and in Sunday School classes, phone calls, and word of mouth are excellent and inexpensive ways to promote the study. Sometimes local radio and television stations announce upcoming events free of charge.

To assist you in promoting the study, we have provided two special promotional segments on tape 1 of the videos included in the leader kit. You may want to preview them now. You will find them at the beginning of the tape before the introductory session. The first segment has been designed for your use inside the church—in a worship service, in a women's Bible-study class, and in other locations where women regularly gather during the week. You have permission to duplicate this segment if you wish to create a loop tape that plays continually. Be sure to have someone prepared to announce the date, time, and place of the introductory session and to invite persons to attend. If the tape is left to play unattended, place a sign beside the monitor that lists the date, time, and place of the introductory session.

The second promotional segment is designed for use in a broadcast situation. You have permission to use it on a local television or cable channel to reach out to your community and invite women to the study. You can purchase a broadcast-quality version of this segment by calling (615) 251-5926 or by emailing *betsy.wedekind@lifeway.com.*

ADJUSTING FOR THE CHURCH CALENDAR

Some churches prefer to offer their Bible-study groups in regular 13-week cycles. The following suggestions will enable you to fit this study into 13 weeks.

- *Week 1.* Conduct an opening/orientation. If you have multiple groups, overview all the different groups that are meeting simultaneously, or just overview *Beloved Disciple.* Include testimonies from a previous Bible study. Possibly include refreshments.
- *Week 2.* Use the introductory session plan, beginning on page 16 in this guide.
- *Weeks 3–12.* Conduct the study as outlined on the following pages.

- *Week 13.* Have a closing celebration with testimonies of changed lives. Share a potluck meal together. Award certificates. Close with a prayer of commitment.

Use your creativity to plan a schedule for this Bible study that will permit maximum participation and opportunity for growth. As you pray and work, the Holy Spirit will lead you to a plan that is right for your ministry.

USING THE MUSIC VIDEO

On videotape 1, immediately after the promotional segment, you will find the music video "Be Thou My Vision." Featuring recording artist Travis Cottrell, the video was taped in Ephesus and on Patmos during the taping of the video sessions. Plan to show it at the close of the introductory session. The stand-alone segment can also be used anytime during the study. Please take four or five minutes to preview the video and consider using it after the introductory session in one or more of these ways.

- Play it at the beginning of each session as a call to worship and Bible study.
- If your group takes a break, play it as a signal to rejoin the group and focus on the Lord.
- Play it during times of reflection and silent prayer.

Use your own creative idea for the music video. We hope you are touched by the Spirit as you view it.

About the Authors

Julie Woodruff, the writer of the leader guide, is an active women's ministry leader in her church and community. She currently leads a community-wide Bible study for women from 20 different churches and 8 denominations.

Julie began the women's ministry at West Conroe Baptist Church in Conroe, Texas, where her husband was the pastor for 13½ years. Julie also taught a women's Sunday School class and Bible study there.

Julie and her husband, Sid, reside in Hendersonville, Tennessee, with their two children, Lauren and Jordan.

Cheris Gaston wrote the retreat plans on pages 11–15. A member of First Baptist Church in Bartlett, Tennessee, Cheris writes worship skits, acts, serves as the director of the adult drama team, and leads a Bible study for women. She is the author of a book of worship scripts, *Under His Direction,* published in 1999. She is a part of "At His Feet," a ministry team of five women who lead Bible studies, skits, games, and music for women's retreats and conferences.

Cheris and her husband, Danny, have two children, Hannah and Seth.

Conducting a Retreat for Beloved Disciple

CHERIS GASTON

The following is a plan for conducting a retreat to launch the study of *Beloved Disciple*. Pray about each detail and decision as you plan this retreat. Adjust these plans to fit your situation and needs.

ENLISTING LEADERS

Enlist a number of leaders to help prepare for and conduct the retreat. By enlisting leaders in advance, you will also spread the word and promote participation. Encourage each leader also to recruit helpers as needed. The following is a list of leaders and their responsibilities.

1. **The Retreat Leader (RL)** is responsible for these tasks.
   - Choose and enlist leaders who can fulfill their duties with servant hearts.
   - Pray for all leaders and participants.
   - Help other leaders when they need assistance.
   - Enlist persons to share testimonies at the retreat.
   - Speak and lead at the retreat at designated times.

2. **The Decorations Leader (DL)** may use the following ideas or create her own.
   - If using tables, cover them with blue or white tablecloths. Place large rocks in the center with netting draped over them and place flowers in the cracks of the rocks. Or wrap the netting around the bottom of the outside of bowls and fill the bowls with water and floating candles.
   - If not using tables, use a large, blue sheet as a backdrop for the meeting area and place large rocks with netting among them as if on a shoreline. Consider painting a ship, clouds, and waves on the backdrop.

3. **The Music Leader (ML)** has the following duties.
   - Provide music that glorifies God and invites worship.
   - Enlist musicians as necessary.
   - Make arrangements for sound equipment.

4. **The Promotional/Games/Skit Leader** (PL, GL, SL) is responsible for carrying out jobs like these.
   - Promote the retreat with signs and announcements providing all necessary information.
   - Enlist people for the skit and lead games.
   - Procure necessary items for promotional activities.

5. **The Food Organizer/Hostess (FO/H)** organizes and provides all food and serving items.

6. **The Written Materials Leader (WML)** makes the following preparation.

- Type material, leaving space for answers.
- Duplicate copies for participants.
- Distribute written materials, pens, pencils, paper, and other items.
- *Optional:* Make a booklet of needed papers in correct order and hand out the booklets at the beginning of the retreat. Also consider a program for participants.

7. **The Photographer** (optional) takes pictures to place in a scrapbook or to promote the next retreat.

8. **All leaders work together to complete these tasks.**
   - Choose a retreat site.
   - Determine fee, keeping food and site expenses in mind.
   - Conduct registration.
   - Prepare and clean up the retreat site.

RETREAT SCHEDULE

FRIDAY NIGHT

1. **Fun by the Shore (WML)**
   WML distributes copies of the game "Fun by the Shore" (p. 14) as participants arrive. (Answers: beloved disciple, near the cross, on the island of Patmos, fisherman, brother of James, writer of Revelation, loved Jesus)

2. **Feeding the Fishermen (RL, FO/H)**
   RL welcomes participants and leads in prayer. FO/H may choose from these suggestions.
   - *Simple:* tuna sandwiches, chips, tea, and cookies
   - *Healthful:* baked fish, green beans, baked potatoes and condiments, garlic bread, tea, and gelatin and/or fresh fruit for dessert
   - *More involved or catered:* fried fish, baked potatoes and condiments or french fries, tossed salad and condiments, tea, and cake decorated to complement the theme: fish, nets, and so forth

3. **A True Promise in a Fish Tail (WML, GL)**
   - This is an icebreaker game. WML makes a very simple drawing of a fish. Duplicate the drawing and write one of the following verses on each fish: Psalm 46:10; Psalm 103:13; John 1:16; John 13:23; Acts 1:8. Duplicate half as many fish as you have participants. Cut each fish into two pieces. Mix up the fish halves and have them ready to distribute.
   - GL says: It's time to begin the fun! Find the person who has the other half of the fish you were handed when you came in. When you find your match,

memorize your verse together and tell each other why you would or would not make good fishermen.

4. Push Out the Boat (RL)

RL says: Thank you for joining us as we set sail on the great adventure God wants us to experience as His disciples. John 10:10 says, " 'I have come that they may have life, and have it to the full.' " We are here to kick off the study of *Beloved Disciple* in an exciting way! When we complete this retreat, we want our hearts and minds to be ready to absorb all the Holy Spirit has to teach us through this study. Now let's share in worship through music.

5. Worship (ML)

ML leads or sings upbeat praise music that is pleasing to the Master Fisherman.

6. A Fisherman's Testimony (RL)

RL enlists someone to share a testimony about the way Jesus changed her life. RL states: As fishermen, we go through different seasons, but the difficult ones prepare us for what is ahead. Peter said, " 'Master, we've worked hard all night and haven't caught anything' " (Luke 5:5). But when Jesus walked up to the boat, everything changed. Both boats were filled with fish. _____ is going to tell us how Jesus walked up to her boat and changed everything in her life.

7. How Much Time Did You Fish? (SL, RL)

- SL enlists five characters:
- —Three women with their backs to the audience— woman 1 holding a remote control, woman 2 holding shopping bags out of view, and woman 3 holding a net out of view
- —A character called Yourself
- —An angel in a white T-shirt with a paper scroll
- SL gives each character a copy of the script "How Much Time Did You Fish?" (p. 14).
- RL introduces skit by saying: The disciples who were fishermen had endured tough times. Endurance would be significant in the ministry they were about to begin. What ministry? Mark 1:17 says, " 'Come follow me and I will make you fishers of men.' " In the following skit, a woman named Yourself enters heaven, and as she talks with an angel, she remembers her life.

8. Net Grippers (WML, RL)

- WML prepares the assignment sheet "Net Grippers" (p. 14) for each small group of from four to eight members.
- RL introduces small-group work by saying: John writes in 1 John 3:1, "How great is the love the Father has lavished on us, that we should be called children of God! And that is what we are!" His love for God is obvious. How close are you to God? Like John, the beloved disciple, do you love Him so much that His will is more important than your own? How strong is your grip on your net? The stronger your love, the stronger your grip. We're going to break into small groups to study our Bibles, pray, and share as each of us looks inside to see how strong our heart for God really is. Are we willing to spend time casting our nets and becoming fishers of men? Break into small groups of from four to eight members each.

9. The Ship Goes to Shore (RL)

RL announces a break time and specifies a time to return.

10. Fishermen Exercises (ML and/or GL)

With fun music playing in the background, ML and/or GL lead participants in doing each of the following motions four or five times. Call out each action.

- Casting your net: use hands and arms as if throwing out a net.
- Raising the sails: pull hands down alternately as if pulling on ropes.
- Swimming: turn your head and bring your left and right arms over alternately.
- Walking on water: like Peter, you've got to have faith—step high!
- Reaching out to others: hug some people.

11. Singing at Sea (ML)

ML leads a sing-along of music that reflects love for Jesus.

12. A Fisherman's Testimony (RL)

RL enlists someone to share a testimony about the way Jesus turned negative circumstances into good in her life. RL states: When Jesus was dying on the cross, which disciple stood there before him? John. And he didn't even understand what was happening. No matter what, we stand by those we love most, and John loved Jesus the most! When you can't explain what Jesus is doing and the net becomes heavy with the burdens of life, stand by faith. Psalm 46:10 says, " 'Be still and know that I am God.' " This study will show how God can take the negative and turn it into a positive. Now _____ is going to share the way God did that in her life.

13. Bound with Prayer (WML, RL)

- WML prepares a copy of the handout "Bound with Prayer" (p. 15) for each person.
- RL introduces the prayer-partners activity by holding up a piece of net and stating: This piece of net is not made up of one simple strand but of many strands crossing each other to make it strong. God loves to hear the prayer of one, but when two or more pray for the same need, that need is bound and saturated in prayer. Sweet fellowship results when two bow in prayer to our Father. Find the person you met with

earlier to form the fish-tail promise. Sit, share, and pray. Instructions have been prepared to guide you.

14. Fishin', Food, and Fellowship (WML, RL, FO/H)

- WML distributes copies of the devotional guide "Can You Cast the Net?" (p. 15) for members to use before breakfast tomorrow morning.
- RL reminds participants to complete the devotional "Can You Cast the Net?" before breakfast. Announce the time to gather in the morning.
- FO/H provides snacks. Options include Goldfish crackers, tropical/fruit punch, bowls of pretzel sticks labeled *fishing poles,* heart-shaped cookies, or cupcakes with heart-shaped sprinkles.

SATURDAY MORNING

1. Time Alone with the Master Fisherman

Participants have personal devotional time, using "Can You Cast the Net?" as a guide.

2. Nourishment for the Adventure (FO/H)

FO/H provides breakfast. Suggestions include bagels, fruit, orange juice, and coffee with condiments.

3. Makin' Waves (ML)

ML provides praise music. Then lead the group to make a wave, as crowds do at ball games, in honor of the King.

4. Tug-of-Net (GL)

GL supplies a large piece of net and a piece of masking tape taped to the floor. Divide six volunteers evenly to make two teams of three. Center the net over the tape and give each team one end of the net. Then let the tug begin. Encourage the audience to cheer. The team that pulls the other team across the tape wins.

5. A Fisherman's Testimony (RL)

RL enlists someone to give a testimony on the joy of seeing someone decide to follow Christ. RL says: Tug-of-Net was fun, but it wasn't just a game. If we magnify the elation the winning team had by one hundred million, we wouldn't come close to knowing what it feels like to enter heaven! Think of this game as a demonstration of what may happen if we don't give up the prejudices our devotional this morning urged us to renounce. Do you remember the way the winning team was pulling the net away from the team that didn't win? If we don't carry the gospel message to others who are unlike us or not on our team, they won't experience the great joy we will have when we meet our Heavenly Father. Instead of pulling away from others, we must love and reach out! I can't begin to imagine how the unsaved will feel on judgment day, but after we read what John has to say in Revelation, each of us should become very burdened for unsaved

individuals. Love God, love others, share the good news of Jesus Christ, and watch the Holy Spirit work. Let's see more souls saved and looking forward to the day they meet their Heavenly Father! Now we're going to hear from a fisherman, _____, who experienced the great joy of seeing someone decide to follow Christ.

6. Not Fish Scales but Heart Scales (WML, RL, ML)

- WML provides a copy of the game sheet "Not Fish Scales but Heart Scales" (p. 15) for each participant. Draw a very large heart with a very small heart inside it at the bottom of the page before copying it. Have scissors ready for participants to use.
- RL hands out copies of the activity and says: These aren't fish scales but truth scales, and the purpose is to examine your love for God and others. Working individually, look at your heart and honestly answer each statement. Circle the number that represents where you are in each area. Finally, pray that God will help you grow to 10 on each scale. Reflect, read, pray, and commit!
- ML provides soft music as members work.
- After members have finished their inventories, RL says: We are the fishermen, but sometimes we need to shed scales or old habits that keep us from loving God with all our hearts. If you have some of these, pray right now that God will help you shed those bad habits. (Pause for silent prayer.) You'll notice a very small heart at the bottom of your paper. Place your finger in it now. Has your love for God been small? Think of your love for God right now and place your whole hand over the large heart. Pray that God's love will consume you and that others will see this love in you every day. (Pause) This retreat's keepsake is nothing fancy. We're going to pass out scissors and let you cut out this large heart. On the back write today's date and the words *Retreat to kick off the study of* Beloved Disciple. Fold the heart and place it in your Bible. Each day of the study, be reminded as you see this heart that like the apostle John, you desire to have a gigantic love for God and those around you.

7. Hearts Revealed (RL)

RL invites anyone who wishes to share or pray.

8. Thank-Yous

RL expresses appreciation to participants and leaders.

9. Closing Prayer (RL)

RL prays that all members will cast their nets for Christ and will open their minds and hearts to learn all that God wants to reveal to them through the upcoming study of *Beloved Disciple: The Life and Ministry of John.*

FUN BY THE SHORE

While waiting for the other fishermen to arrive, unscramble these words to describe the apostle John.

1. levdobe elisdpci

   _____

2. rnae eth sorcs (John 19:25-26)

   _____

3. on het disnla fo soPtam (Rev. 1:9)

   _____

4. iemfsnhra (Mark 1:16-20)

   _____

5. orrhteb fo emJsa (Matt. 4:21)

   _____

6. rewitr fo neevRltoia (Rev. 1:1)

   _____

7. voled suseJ (John 14:21)

   _____

NET GRIPPERS

1. Think of a time when you felt it was difficult to do God's will. Share with your small group if you would like to do so. Read Hebrews 10:36. Someone pray that each of you can persevere in difficulties and complete His will at whatever cost.

2. To do God's will, we must be draped with humility. Think of and share situations in which Christians have difficulty being humble. Read 2 Chronicles 7:14. Someone pray that your group will not be puffed up by egos but will be humbled in light of His glory and grace.

3. Can you think of times you didn't cast your net and become a fisher of men? Share if you would like to. Was it because of fear? Read Psalm 56:3. Someone pray that in future opportunities each of you will have the courage, passion, and sensitivity to cast your net.

HOW MUCH TIME DID YOU FISH?

Yourself: (*agitated*) What do you mean, Angel?

Angel: Yourself, I'm asking you how much time you spent fishing. OK, let me put it another way. Tell me what symbol would best represent how you spent most of your time on earth.

Yourself: I still don't understand what you mean!

Angel: Well, maybe some visual reminders will help. *Opens scroll. Woman 1 turns around and begins clicking the remote.* You enjoyed watching television for yourself approximately 27,498 hours. *Woman 2 turns around and begins walking in place, swinging shopping bags.* You enjoyed shopping and buying for yourself approximately 8,321 hours. *Woman 3 turns around holding net. Angel reads sadly but with emphasis.* And being a fisherman for the cause of Christ … only 17 hours. *Angel closes scroll, kindly puts hand on Yourself's shoulder. Yourself sadly walks over to women 1 and 2, takes the remote control, places it in a shopping bag, and hands the bags to Angel.*

Yourself: Honestly, my time was mostly spent with these. *Takes net from woman 3.* Now I see it all so clearly, but now it's too late. *Wraps net around woman 3.* If only I'd done His will instead of mine, I could have spent more time doing this. *Bends on one knee and bows head. Others exit.*

BOUND WITH PRAYER

1. Record your prayer partner's name and phone number:

   _____

   Share with each other about your backgrounds, vocations, families, and interests.
2. Share with each other personal, family, and service-related prayer requests. Record your partner's requests here.

   _____

   _____

   _____
3. Set a time each week you can call and pray with each other or think of a time each week each of you can pause to pray for the other:_____ Don't forget to call each other when prayers are answered!
4. Pause now and pray for each other.

NOT FISH SCALES BUT HEART SCALES

	Low	High
I know that God loves me.		1 2 3 4 5 6 7 8 9 10
I love God with all my heart.		1 2 3 4 5 6 7 8 9 10
I love others who are not like me.		1 2 3 4 5 6 7 8 9 10
I desire to share God's love with others.		1 2 3 4 5 6 7 8 9 10
I seek to do God's will in my life.		1 2 3 4 5 6 7 8 9 10

Pray for 10s! Reevaluate yourself every few months. Pray for God to circumcise your heart to love Him. Praise Him as you see heart change in your responses.

CAN YOU CAST THE NET?

Loving others can be difficult when we have prejudices against certain groups of people. Take an honest inventory of your heart and check the groups or individuals you find most difficult to love.

❏ poor	❏ other religions	❏ disadvantaged
❏ arrogant	❏ atheists	❏ unattractive
❏ handicapped	❏ other sexual preferences	❏ attractive
❏ old	❏ young	❏ coworkers
❏ unforgiving	❏ strangers	❏ foreigners
❏ other skin colors	❏ abusive	❏ family members
❏ wealthy	❏ unloving	❏ sick
❏ angry	❏ neighbors	❏ other _____

Read 1 John 4:7-21. How many times do you see the word *love?* _____ John wrote about God's love, our love for God, and our love for our brother. We will not be able to cast the nets effectively if we don't passionately have all three!
1. As you study Scripture, it will assure you that you have God's love!
2. As you get to know Christ, your love for Him will grow.
3. Pray that your love for God and others will increase to such an intensity that you will long to cast the net—sharing God's Word and His love!

Introductory Session

PLAN A

BEFORE THE SESSION

1. If you expect 20 or more participants, set up tables with cards indicating a division of the alphabet at several stations. For example, those with last names beginning with letters A–E will sign up at one station, F–J at the next, and so forth.

2. Enlist a volunteer or small-group leader to sit at each station. Designate those each leader registers as members of her group. Adjustments will need to be made where numbers fall unevenly.

3. Each registrar, whether a leader or a volunteer, should be at her station 30 minutes before registration is to begin. Each should be equipped with member books, registration cards or sign-up sheets (drawn up by your church or study leader), pens, and name tags.

4. Each registrar assumes responsibility for members' first impression. She needs to wear her name tag, be ready to greet new members with enthusiasm, anticipate questions with knowledgeable answers, make participants feel welcome, and tell them what to do next. (After registration members will report to the joint session for the introductory segment. After this first introductory meeting, members will begin each week in their large groups for welcome, worship, and prayer.)

DURING THE SESSION

Introduction to *Beloved Disciple* (60 mins.)

1. Open the introductory session with prayer.

2. Welcome members and introduce leaders. If your group is small, have each member introduce herself. You may want to create an icebreaker.

3. After introductions, give instructions and information about the course. Include the following points.

   a. Have members scan the first week's daily assignments in the member book. Explain that they are to complete a week of study before each group session. Emphasize that although the daily assignments are crucial, members should attend the weekly sessions even if their work is incomplete. Tell them to expect each daily assignment to take about 45 minutes.

   b. Encourage members to read the introduction in the member book before beginning their study.

   c. Using the introduction to week 1 as an example, explain that the format is designed to enhance learning. Point out that the Principle Questions, listed in the introduction to each week, and the Personal Discussion Questions, appearing with the symbol ⌷, will be discussed in weekly sessions.

   d. Emphasize that the primary purposes of small-group discussion are—

   • accountability. In-depth Bible studies are most often completed successfully in a group.

   • to underscore basic biblical truths. This will be accomplished through discussing answers to the Principle Questions, which ensure that the week's content has been received and understood.

   • to personally apply the study. This will be accomplished through discussing answers to the Personal Discussion Questions.

   e. Express the need to be good stewards of time. Ask members to adopt these time guidelines.

   • Leaders: Be early each week!

   • Members: Be on time each week!

   • Small groups: Start on time! Leaders must start on time regardless of the number present.

   • Members: Your personal comments are vital to the discussion time, but please make them brief.

4. Announce that after today's introductory meeting, members will participate in a small group each week as well as a large group. Tell them they will receive a call within 24 hours identifying their leader and telling where their group will meet for discussion of sessions 1–10. Allow 45 minutes for small-group discussion divided according to the following schedule.

   • Prayer requests and prayer (5 mins.). Ask that prayer requests be stated in one brief sentence. Graciously intervene if a request becomes lengthy.

   • Discussion of Principle Questions and Personal Discussion Questions (40 mins.). Allow 7–8 minutes to discuss each day's assignment. Each day's Principle Question can be answered in 2–3 minutes, leaving 5–6 minutes for the Personal Discussion Question. Write these time divisions on a marker board for all members to keep in mind and adhere to.

Introductory Video Presentation (50 mins.)

Each week after the group discussion, gather members in a joint session to view the video that enhances and concludes each unit. Take 5 minutes for the transition. The video presentation will be from 45 to 50 minutes.

Closing Remarks and Prayer (5 mins.)

Share closing comments and briefly introduce week 1. Ask members to complete week 1 before the next session.

AFTER THE SESSION

1. Compile all registration cards and, if there are more than 12 members and more than 1 leader, divide the list of members into small groups. These discussion groups need to be a maximum of 12 members.

2. Have leader(s) call members within the next 24 hours to introduce themselves and tell them where their group will meet the following week.

3. Have a leader or a volunteer create attendance sheets from the registration cards so that every leader can take roll in each session. These attendance sheets need to be given to each leader prior to the next session.

PLAN B

BEFORE THE SESSION

1. Be prepared to register members. Have member books, registration cards or sign-up sheets, pens, and name tags. Assume responsibility for new members' first impression. Wear a name tag, be ready to greet members with enthusiasm, anticipate questions with knowledge-able answers, make participants feel welcome, and invite them to take a seat.

2. Have a praise CD or cassette playing as members enter the room. If desired, have light refreshments available.

DURING THE SESSION

1. Open the introductory session with prayer.

2. Welcome members and introduce yourself. Ask each member to introduce herself by stating her name, iden-tifying the person in her life who has loved her most, and explaining how she knows that is true. State that we will study the life and ministry someone who called himself "the disciple whom Jesus loved" (John 21:7). Ask someone to quote or read John 3:16. State: John the apostle knew that Jesus loved him because He came to give His life for him and for the whole world. Our goal is to discover the depths of Christ's love for us through the writings of John, the beloved disciple.

3. Give instructions and information about the course, including the following points.

   a. Have members scan the first week's daily assign-ments in the member book. Explain that they are to complete a week of study before each group session.
   Emphasize that although the daily assignments are crucial, members should attend the weekly sessions even if their work is incomplete. Tell them to expect each daily assignment to take about 45 minutes.

   b. Encourage members to read the introduction in the member book before beginning their study.

   c. Using the introduction to week 1 as an example, explain that the format is designed to enhance learn-ing. Point out that the Principle Questions, listed in the introduction to each week, and the Personal Discussion Questions, appearing with the symbol ⬧, highlight key points in each week's material.

   d. Emphasize that the primary purposes of each week's group discussion are—

   • accountability. In-depth Bible studies are most often completed successfully in a group.

   • to underscore basic biblical truths. This will be accomplished through discussion and group learning activities, which ensure that the week's content has been received and understood.

   • to personally apply the study. This will be accom-plished through particular activities in the session.

   e. Express the need to be good stewards of the time for each session. Ask participants to to be on time for each session. Emphasize that although each person's comments are vital to the discussion time, members should make them brief.

4. Announce that after today's introductory meeting, members will follow this schedule each week.

   • Welcome, prayer, and discussion (50 mins.). State that members will be allowed to request prayer. Ask that prayer requests be stated in one brief sentence. Then the group will discuss the week's content.

   • Break and return to group (10 mins.). Ask the group whether it would like to have light refreshments and beverages each week during this break. If so, decide how this will be done.

   • View video segment (50 mins.). Explain that the video presentation, which will be from 45 to 50 min-utes, enhances and concludes each unit of study.

   • Closing assignment and prayer (5 mins.). Explain that you will close each session by reminding members of their at-home assignment and by having prayer.

5. Share closing comments. Briefly introduce week 1. Ask members to complete week 1 before the next session.

6. Close by praying that members will experience Christ's love as never before through their study of John. Collect name tags as the group departs.

VIDEO RESPONSE SHEET

Introductory Group Session

As we begin a journey that will take us throughout Galilee into Samaria, to Jerusalem, to Ephesus, and to Patmos, let's consider adopting the same invitations for embarkation that John encountered.

Read John 1:35-51.

1. Let's sense Christ asking us the same question: "___*[Your name]*___, My child, what do you want?

   What are you seeking here and now in this _____ _____ of your life?"

2. Let's be willing to "_____ _____ _____."

3. Consider the unfathomable grace of God that we sometimes "find" Christ when we didn't even know

   _____ was the_____ we were _____ _____.

4. We will miss untold treasures if we confuse "_____ ___ _____"

   with "_____ ____ _____."

5. Let's begin our journey as a true seeker "in whom there is _____ _____."

6. Wherever we've recently _____, Jesus has _____ ___ _____.

7. As Christ reveals how He has "_____" _____, our eyes are somehow

   _____ to "see" _____.

By design, no answers are provided for these blanks.

Fresh Winds over Galilee

SESSION 1

PLAN A

BEFORE THE SESSION

1. Complete all of week 1 in the member book.
2. Pray that each member will be teachable and that God will reveal Himself through this study.
3. Pray for God's guidance in your preparation.
4. Carefully read "During the Session."
5. Arrange the room to create an intimate setting for your group. If you have a group of 12 or under, arrange the chairs in a tight circle. If you have more than 12, two tight semicircles will work well.
6. If you are using the video, do the following.
   - Make sure all arrangements have been made to secure and set up necessary equipment in the room.
   - Preview the video and fill in your response sheet in the member book. This step will be beneficial to you in case you are detained or distracted with administrative duties as members watch the video.
   - Prepare several sentences in response to the video.

**Child Care Open, Attendance
and Homework Check (15 mins.)**

DURING THE SESSION

Large Group—Welcome, Worship, and Prayer (15 mins.)
1. Greet members as they arrive and hand out name tags.
2. Lead a time of worship and praise.
3. Pray, asking for God's presence and blessing.
4. Dismiss to small groups.

Small Groups (45 mins.)
1. Ask for prayer requests and have prayer (5 mins.).
2. Review the week's Principle Questions and Personal Discussion Questions (40 mins.).

Look for brief (two- or three-minute) answers to the Principle Questions so that you can be satisfied that the material was understood. All answers should have been obvious as the reading and the learning activities of week 1 were completed; however, make sure you have written answers in case members do not volunteer or understand.

Each day's Principle Question will be followed by a Personal Discussion Question, which is identified in each day's study by the symbol ✿. Give members the opportunity to answer, but do not pressure them. Ask them to be discreet and never to name another person who could be hurt by the discussion. Appropriate discussion of these questions is key to the application of the session. Be ready to redirect discussion if it becomes inappropriate.

Day 1
- *Principle Question:* What was John the Baptist's purpose for preaching?
- *Personal Discussion:* Can you relate? On the set of scales in the margin indicate where your balance lies between relationship and legalism.

Day 2
- *Principle Question:* How was John identified in his family?
- *Personal Discussion:* How would you explain to a new Christian the relationship between the things of God and the things of family?

Day 3
- *Principle Question:* What name did Simon call Jesus in Luke 5:5?
- *Personal Discussion:* At this season of your life, what do you sense that you need most?
   - ❏ Preparation for a fresh work of God
   - ❏ Repairing from a tear
   - ❏ Restoration from a kind of fall

Day 4
- *Principle Question:* How did Christ build His new followers?
- *Personal Discussion:* How do you picture Christ's expression and demeanor as He called these four fishermen to follow Him? Briefly explain.

Day 5
- *Principle Question:* According to Mark 1:25-26, what happened when Jesus commanded the demons to come out of the man?

• *Personal Discussion:* What kinds of feelings did you have the last time you encountered someone who was suffering terribly?

If time allows, ask for ways God spoke in week 1.

Conclude the 40-minute discussion time by thanking and affirming members. If you are using the video, do so at this time. If not, dismiss with a few introductory words about week 2 and a closing prayer. Take the 5 remaining minutes in the first hour to prepare for the video.

Break and Return to Large Group (5 mins.)

View Video Presentation 1 (50 mins.)

Closing Assignment and Prayer (5 mins.)
1. Give a brief response to the video.
2. Briefly introduce week 2 and encourage members to complete the study before the next session.
3. Close with prayer and collect name tags.

AFTER THE SESSION
1. Immediately record concerns or impressions you had to pray for members. Pray for these throughout the week.
2. Evaluate session 1 by asking yourself the following questions and recording your answers.
   • Was I adequately prepared for today's session?
   • Did I begin and end session 1 on time? If not, how can I help make sure our time is used more wisely in session 2?
   • Does anyone need extra encouragement this week? Follow up with a card or a phone call, if appropriate.
   • What was my overall impression of session 1?
3. Read "Before the Session" on page 19 to learn what preparations you need to make for session 2.

PLAN B

BEFORE THE SESSION
1. Spend time in prayer for those in your group.
2. Provide tear sheets, markers, and tape for group work.
3. Write the following small-group assignments on index cards: *Group 1: Matthew 4:18-22. Group 2: Mark 1:14-20. Group 3: Luke 5:1-11.*
4. Have praise music playing as group members arrive.

Child Care Open, Attendance and Homework Check (15 mins.)

DURING THE SESSION

Welcome, Prayer, and Discussion (50 mins.)
1. Welcome group members and check homework as they arrive. Encourage group members to introduce themselves to someone they don't know.
2. Lead the group in a time of prayer.
3. Discuss the illustration on page 9. Ask: What is the difference between relationship and legalism? Where does your balance lie?
4. Instruct members to form pairs and to read Luke 3:1-9 together. Discuss what it must have been like to hear the Word of God after four hundred years of silence.
5. Ask a volunteer to read Deuteronomy 6:4-9. As a group, list the priorities God delivered in this directive. Describe the relationship between the things of God and the things of family.
6. Divide into triads. Ask them to list facts about John. Then have them share their lists with the entire group and combine them to make a complete list on a marker board or on a tear sheet.
7. Divide into three groups and give them tear sheets, markers, and the index cards with Scripture references. Ask groups to read their assigned Scriptures and to record on their tear sheets facts about Jesus' calling His disciples. Then allow each group to share its findings with the entire group. Compare each list and circle facts that are unique to each Gospel.
8. Discuss the questions on pages 20–21. Keep the discussion moving so that you will not run out of time. The purpose is to hear different ideas on how group members perceive Christ and His followers.
9. What were the things that attracted Peter, Andrew, James, and John to Jesus? List responses on a marker board or on a tear sheet on the wall.
10. Discuss as a group what impact the events discussed in day 5 might have had on John.

Break and Return to Group (10 mins.)

View Video Segment 1 (50 mins.)

Closing Assignment and Prayer (5 mins.)
11. Remind members of the letters Beth asked them to write telling Christ what they are seeking most through this study. Challenge members to continue praying for these desires throughout the study.
12. Ask members to complete their daily assignments in week 2 before the next group session.
13. Dismiss with prayer that during this study each member will distinctly hear Jesus' call on her life.

VIDEO RESPONSE SHEET

Group Session 1

Sometimes we also may have the desire to take our _____ **whips** _____ and

_____ **turn** _____ **over** _____ **the** _____ **tables** _____ in our worlds: in our ____ **children's** ____

_____ **schools** _____, in our _____ **communities** _____, in our _____ **churches** _____, etc. We've got to

be so careful what we rationalize by Scripture. Before we proceed, we are wise to remember a few

important things. We'll make six points today based on the calling of John.

Read Mark 3:13-19 and John 2:12-17.

1. Christ could not ____ **sin** ____ in His _____ **zeal** _____ or _____ **anger** _____. **See Ephesians 4:26-27.**

   Anger and rage are highly motivational, but they are extremely destructive.

2. Godly _____ **indignation** _____ is measured by the _____ **absence** _____ of " _____ **self** _____."

3. God looks upon the _____ **heart** _____ beneath the action. We can even have a

   _____ **wrong** _____ _____ **heart** _____ about a _____ **right** _____ _____ **issue** _____ and

   find ourselves disciplined by God.

4. Paradoxically, we receive our calling as ____ **one** ____ **kind** ____ **of** ____ **person** _____

   but can only fulfill it ____ **as** ____ _____ **another** _____. **See Matthew 18:2-3.** "Unless you change and

   become _____ *[your answer]* _____, you will never _____ *[your answer]* _____

   _____ *[your answer]* _____.' "

5. Though _____ **preparation** _____ is important, Christ seems to have an affinity for

   _____ **on-the-job** _____ _____ **training** _____.

6. The kind of change God desires comes one primary way. **See Mark 3:14:** "that they might

   be with him and that he might send them out."

Sights and Insights

SESSION 2

PLAN A

BEFORE THE SESSION

Refer to page 19 for a list of preparatory actions.

Child Care Open, Attendance and Homework Check (15 mins.)

DURING THE SESSION

Large Group—Welcome, Worship, and Prayer (15 mins.)
1. Greet members and hand out name tags.
2. Lead a time of worship and praise.
3. Pray, asking for God's presence and blessing.
4. Dismiss to small groups.

Small Groups (45 mins.)
1. Ask for prayer requests and have prayer (5 mins.).
2. Review the week's Principle Questions and Personal Discussion Questions (40 mins.).

Look for brief answers to the Principle Questions that will indicate the comprehension of the reading and learning activities in week 2. Be prepared to offer the answer if a member does not volunteer. Also be prepared to keep personal discussion within appropriate bounds.

Day 1
- *Principle Question:* According to John 11:41-42, what confidence did Christ have in His praying?
- *Personal Discussion:* How differently would we pray if we were convinced of two critical factors: that our Father is the omnipotent Creator and Sustainer of the universe and that He always hears us?

Day 2
- *Principle Question:* Based on Mark 5:35, what was the reasoning of those who discouraged Jairus from bothering the teacher anymore?
- *Personal Discussion:* Where has God taken you personally to transfigure your perception of Him?

Day 3
- *Principle Question:* What is the obvious risk of great revelation, and how are we told in 2 Corinthians 12:7 that God safeguarded the apostle Paul against it?

- *Personal Discussion:* Under the Holy Spirit's inspiration, what did Paul pray for us (see Eph. 1:17)?

Day 4
- *Principle Question:* Based on Luke 19:41-44, why was Jesus apparently so grief-stricken?
- *Personal Discussion:* Read James 3:13-16. Why do you think humility is so wise?

Day 5
- *Principle Question:* What happened as soon as Judas took the bread at the Passover?
- *Personal Discussion:* When was the last time you saw someone you consider to be a rock in unabashed anguish, virtually inconsolable, and overwhelmed with sorrow? Describe how you felt.

If time allows, ask for ways God spoke in week 2.

Conclude the 40-minute discussion time by thanking and affirming members. If you are using the video, do so now. If not, dismiss with a few introductory words about week 3 and a closing prayer.

Break and Return to Large Group (5 mins.)

View Video Presentation 2 (50 mins.)

Closing Assignment and Prayer (5 mins.)
1. Give a brief response to the video.
2. Briefly introduce week 3 and encourage members to complete the study before the next session.
3. Close with prayer and collect name tags.

AFTER THE SESSION
1. Immediately record concerns or impressions you had to pray for members. Pray for these throughout the week.
2. Evaluate session 2 by asking yourself the following questions and recording your answers.
   - Was I adequately prepared for today's session?
   - Did I begin and end session 2 on time? If not, how can I make sure our time is used more wisely in session 3?
   - Does anyone need extra encouragement this week? Follow up with a card or a phone call, if appropriate.
   - What was my overall impression of session 2?

3. Read "Before the Session" on page 19 to learn what preparations you need to make for session 3.

PLAN B

BEFORE THE SESSION

1. Write group assignments on index cards for activity 5. *Group 1: Matthew 17:1-9. Group 2: Mark 9:2-10. Group 3: Luke 9:28-36.*
2. Provide tear sheets, markers, and tape for group work.
3. Have praise music playing as group members arrive.

Child Care Open, Attendance and Homework Check (15 mins.)

DURING THE SESSION
Group Session—Welcome, Prayer, and Discussion (50 mins.)

1. Have group members form pairs with the person sitting beside them. Ask them to introduce themselves to each other if they are not already acquainted and to tell something about themselves. Then they should share prayer requests with each other and pray.
2. Ask a volunteer to read Mark 1:29-39. Recap what has occurred in the past 24 hours with Jesus and the disciples.
3. Ask for volunteers to reveal their favorite places for prayer. Ask each, What makes that place work for you?
4. Ask the group to discuss the assignment on page 33. Ask whether members prayed, beginning with John 11:42, " 'I knew that you always hear me,' " and concluded with John 11:41: " 'Father, I thank you that you have heard me.' " Share testimonies about practicing God's presence.
5. Divide into three groups and give each group an index card with a Scripture reference. Direct groups to read their verses and record details of the passages on tear sheets. Then ask groups to share with the entire group. As reports are given, hang tear sheets on the wall. Circle the information that differs in each account and underline the information that is the same.
6. As a group, answer the questions on page 38: "What did they discuss as they came down the mountain? Why do you think Jesus let the three disciples follow Him to Jairus' house and to the transfiguration? What points do you think He was trying to make to Peter, James, and John? What do Jesus' actions say to you today?"
7. Ask small groups to read Mark 10:35-45 and to answer this question: In what ways do we ascribe to the same philosophy of spiritual toddlerhood that James and John had? Ask them to make lists to share with the large group.
8. Ask members to share ways Satan has betrayed them. Remind them to be general with their answers. Record on a marker board or on a tear sheet a list of words that describe ways Satan has betrayed them.
9. As a group, make a list of what Jesus represented to the disciples for the three years they followed Him. Write the list on a marker board or on a tear sheet.
10. Ask, What emotions do you think Peter, James, and John felt as they watched Jesus struggle in the garden of Gethsemane?

Break and Return to Group (10 mins.)

View Video Segment 2 (50 mins.)

Closing Assignment and Prayer (5 mins.)
11. Ask members to complete their daily assignments in week 3 before the next group session.
12. Referring to the list of what Jesus represented to the disciples, close in prayer thanking Jesus for being those things to members, as well.

VIDEO RESPONSE SHEET

Group Session 2

Reflect on John 18:15-18,25-27.

1. Few experiences lend more opportunity to be ____*disappointed*____ by someone we've

____*highly*____ ____*esteemed*____ than a traumatic event.

2. Each of us is wise to ask the following question: Who have I given enough ____*power*____

to ___*throw*___ ___*me*___ ___*off*___ ___*course*___ by his or her ____*denial-like*____ actions toward Christ?

3. Sudden uncharacteristic actions do not by themselves render the person or ministry ____*fraudulent*____.

See 2 Corinthians 11:2-3.

4. Wise is the man or woman who realizes he or she, too, could momentarily ___*deny*___ Christ. May we

never ___*withhold*___ from ___*another*___ something that—in due time—we may ___*desperately*___ ___*need*___.

Read John 18:28-31,38-40; 19:12-16.

1. Chaotic events don't place us suddenly out of control nearly as much as they remind us how

____*little*____ ____*control*____ we had ___*all*___ ___*along*___. **See 2 Thessalonians 2:3.**

2. When we feel tremendously ___*out*___ ___*of*___ ____*control*____ in one area, without God's help

we will ordinarily ____*transfer*____ a ____*tighter*____ ____*control-grip*____ on another area.

3. We will never develop ____*authentic*____ ____*confidence*____ in God's sovereign control

until we let Him ___*see*___ ___*us*___ ___*through*___ ____*seasons*____ when life seems out of control.

4. Keep in mind that Satan's first goal in a believer's life in trauma is to encourage

____*cessation*____ of ____*communication*____ with God.

5. God may not always answer ___*our*___ ____*questions*____, but He will always ____*answer*____ ___*us*___.

Psalm 65:5: "You answer us with awesome ____*deeds*____ of ____*righteousness*____, O God our Savior."

Jeremiah 33:3: " ' "Call to me and I will answer you and tell you ____*great*____ and

____*unsearchable*____ ____*things*____ ___*you*___ ___*do*___ ___*not*___ ____*know*____." ' "

Psalm 69:13: "O God, answer me with your ____*sure*____ ____*salvation*____."

Defining Moments

SESSION 3

PLAN A

BEFORE THE SESSION

Refer to page 19 for a list of preparatory actions.

Child Care Open, Attendance and Homework Check (15 mins.)

DURING THE SESSION

Large Group—Welcome, Worship, and Prayer (15 mins.)
1. Greet members and hand out name tags.
2. Lead a time of worship and praise.
3. Pray, asking for God's presence and blessing.
4. Dismiss to small groups.

Small Groups (45 mins.)
1. Ask for prayer requests and have prayer (5 mins.).
2. Review the week's Principle Questions and Personal Discussion Questions (40 mins.).

Day 1
- *Principle Question:* Based on what you studied in day 1, how would you describe John?
- *Personal Discussion:* What thoughts might have gone through John's mind as he heard the verdict?

Day 2
- *Principle Question:* According to Ephesians 1:19-20, what does God promise us if we keep believing?
- *Personal Discussion:* Read John 19:28-30. Reflect on the events of the previous 3 years for John and 33 years for Mary. What kinds of feelings do you think they might have experienced?

Day 3
- *Principle Question:* Based on Acts 1:3, what length of time did Christ use to reveal Himself after He rose from the dead?
- *Personal Discussion:* Have you jumped out of the boat of the comfortable and acceptable? Do you want Jesus even if you have to make a fool of yourself to get to Him? If so, elaborate. If not, what's holding you back?

Day 4
- *Principle Question:* In Acts 1:8 what did Jesus tell His followers they would receive?
- *Personal Discussion:* Think of several reasons God may have for not telling His followers (both past and present) the times and dates of the kingdom.

Day 5
- *Principle Question:* What does Galatians 3:29 say about you?
- *Personal Discussion:* Have you ever begged for something that you realize would have done nothing but help keep you in your crippled estate?

If time allows, ask for ways God spoke in week 3.

Conclude the 40-minute discussion time by thanking and affirming members. If you are using the video, do so now. If not, dismiss with a few introductory words about week 4 and a closing prayer.

Break and Return to Large Group (5 mins.)

View Video Presentation 3 (50 mins.)

Closing Assignment and Prayer (5 mins.)
1. Give a brief response to the video.
2. Briefly introduce week 4 and encourage members to complete the study before the next session.
3. Close with prayer and collect name tags.

AFTER THE SESSION
1. Immediately record concerns or impressions you had to pray for members. Pray for these throughout the week.
2. Evaluate session 3 by asking yourself the following questions and recording your answers.
   - Was I adequately prepared for today's session?
   - Did I begin and end session 3 on time? If not, how can I help make sure our time is used more wisely in session 4?
   - Does anyone need extra encouragement this week? Follow up with a card or a phone call, if appropriate.
   - What was my overall impression of session 3?
3. Read "Before the Session" on page 19 to learn what preparations you need to make for session 4.

PLAN B

BEFORE THE SESSION

1. Arrange for someone in the group or someone you know to sing the hymn "Were You There?"
2. Have a wooden cross made that is big enough and thick enough for group members to drive nail into.
3. Bring hammers, nails, and small slips of paper for activity 2.
4. Prepare the following assignment sheets.

   Group 1. Read John 21:1-14 and answer the following questions: Who was in the boat? When did Jesus appear on the shore? What question did He ask? What did He suggest they do? What was the result? What did John say? How did Peter respond? What did the rest of the disciples do? When they arrived on shore, what did Jesus do for them? How did the disciples know it was Jesus? How would you have responded if you had been a part of the group? As a group, decide what is the most significant part of the account.

   Group 2. Read John 21:15-23 and answer the following questions: What three questions did Jesus ask Peter? How did Peter respond? What did Christ say to Peter in verse 19? What was the obvious motivation for which Christ wanted Peter to follow Him? Where was John while Jesus and Peter were talking? When Peter saw John, what did he ask? What do you think was the tone in Peter's voice when he asked the question? Share testimonies of similar experiences when group members have asked, "Lord what about him?" What was Christ's response to Peter in verse 22?

5. Write the following definition on a tear sheet to display during the session: `ahar: after, later, behind, following.`
6. Provide tear sheets and markers for group activities.

Child Care Open, Attendance and Homework Check (15 mins.)

DURING THE SESSION

Group Session—Welcome, Prayer, and Discussion (50 mins.)

1. Play praise music as members arrive.
2. Place the cross at the front of the room. Hand out slips of paper and ask group members to write a besetting sin on the paper and fold it. State that this is a time of worship. Explain that in a moment, after the song is sung, the group members are to quietly make their way to the front and nail their sins to the cross. Ask that members remain silent during this time as they reflect on the price Jesus paid for their sins. Turn off the lights as the enlisted person sings "Were You There?" As facilitator, begin the procession to the cross to show them members to do. After all members have nailed their sins to the cross, spend time thanking God for sending His Son into the world to die for our sins.
3. Allow volunteers to share testimonies of what the worship experience meant to them.
4. As a group, discuss what might have gone through John's mind as he heard the verdict "Crucify Him!"
5. Ask a volunteer to read John 19:28-30 and discuss the question on page 56: "Reflect on the events of the previous 3 years for John and 33 years for Mary. What kinds of feelings do you think they might have experienced?"
6. Have group members close their eyes and ask them to imagine the scene you are about to read to them. Ask them to place themselves somewhere in the scene and to picture all the details. Read John 20:1-18 slowly and with emotion so that the group can get the picture. Discuss what group members felt and saw as they put themselves in the account.
7. Divide members into two groups and give them the assignment sheets you prepared. Allow time for work and ask each group to share with the entire group.
8. As a group, search Acts 1:1—2:21 and put together a chronological order of the significant events. List these on a marker board or on a tear sheet on the wall.
9. Ask volunteers to share what they wrote about the early church in the activity on page 67.
10. Display the definition of the Hebrew word for *future.* Ask, If we are going to become the effective servants God desires us to be, what is the balance between our past and our future?

Break and Return to Group (10 mins.)

View Video Segment 3 (50 mins.)

Closing Assignment and Prayer (5 mins.)

11. Ask members to complete their daily assignments in week 4 before the next group session.
12. Close with prayer thanking God for the miracles you have seen this week in His Word and asking Him for faith to let Him change us.

VIDEO RESPONSE SHEET

Group Session 3

Read Acts 4:23-32.

The Greek word *deesis* refers to a ____*particular*____ ____*need*____ for which one prays.

How did God respond to their prayers?

- The place where they were meeting was ____*shaken*____. The Greek word means "to move

   to and fro, shake … to put into a state of waving, ____*rocking*____, vibratory motion."

- They were __*all*__ filled with the Holy Spirit.

- They __*all*__ spoke the Word of God boldly.

1. They neither ____*denied*____ nor ____*minimized*____ the seriousness of the problem (v. 23).

2. The believers ____*united*____ for prayer in a way God highly honors. (The Greek word is *homothumadon*.)

   - *Homos* means ____*one*____ and the ____*same*____.

   - *Thumos* means __*temperament*__, ____*mind*____. Also, "With one mind, with __*unanimous*__

      ____*consent*____, in one accord, all together." *Thumos* can also mean ____*passion*____

   as well as mind or thought.

   If God honors His people coming together with ONE MIND and passion, whose mind is right?

   Philippians 2:5 (KJV) says, "Let ____*this*____ ____*mind*____ be in you, which was also

   in ____*Christ*____ ____*Jesus*____." What kind of mind did He have?

   - He made Himself of __*no*__ ____*reputation*____.

   - He took on the ____*form*____ ____*of*____ ____*a*____ ____*servant*____.

   - He ____*humbled*____ Himself. Proverbs 13:10 says, "Pride only breeds quarrels."

3. They corporately ____*exalted*____ God. In doing so, they ____*glorified*____ Him and reminded

   themselves to whom ____*they*____ ____*belonged*____ (Acts 4:24).

4. They cited ____*Scripture*____ ____*relevant*____ to their challenge (vv. 25-26).

5. They reminded themselves that anything God allows to ____*threaten*____ ____*His*____ ____*own*____,
   He will use to bring about great glory.

6. Then they asked ____*big*____ ____*things*____.

Beyond the Limits

SESSION 4

PLAN A

BEFORE THE SESSION

Refer to page 19 for a list of preparatory actions.

Child Care Open, Attendance and Homework Check (15 mins.)

DURING THE SESSION

Large Group—Welcome, Worship, and Prayer (15 mins.)
1. Greet members and hand out name tags.
2. Lead a time of worship and praise.
3. Pray, asking for God's presence and blessing.
4. Dismiss to small groups.

Small Groups (45 mins.)
1. Ask for prayer requests and have prayer (5 mins.).
2. Review the week's Principle Questions and Personal Discussion Questions (40 mins.).

Day 1
- *Principle Question:* According to John 4:9, what was the situation at the time of the disciples' ministry?
- *Personal Discussion:* How has God allowed something to push down your fence so that He could expand your horizon?

Day 2
- *Principle Question:* Why might John have been with Christ's biological family?
- *Personal Discussion:* Would you be willing to live— and die—alone with Christ?

Day 3
- *Principle Question:* How do we know from Paul's testimony that John held a primary role in the Christian church in Jerusalem (see Gal. 2:9)?
- *Personal Discussion:* Who has extended you a hand of fellowship and how? Or to whom have you graciously extended one and how?

Day 4
- *Principle Question:* According to Hebrews 2:14-15, what kind of freedom did Christ give us?
- *Personal Discussion:* When you're weak, down, or tired, doesn't Satan occasionally try to awaken old temptations in you? If so, how?

Day 5
- *Principle Question:* How do you imagine John felt as the solitary remaining apostle?
- *Personal Discussion:* Are you desperate for a surplus of love and acceptance? If so, tell why.

If time allows, ask for ways God spoke in week 4.

Conclude the 40-minute discussion time by thanking and affirming members. If you are using the video, do so now. If not, dismiss with a few introductory words about week 5 and a closing prayer.

Break and Return to Large Group (5 mins.)

View Video Presentation 4 (50 mins.)

Closing Assignment and Prayer (5 mins.)
1. Give a brief response to the video.
2. Briefly introduce week 5 and encourage members to complete the study before the next session.
3. Close with prayer and collect name tags.

AFTER THE SESSION
1. Immediately record concerns or impressions you had to pray for members. Pray for these throughout the week.
2. Evaluate session 4 by asking yourself the following questions and recording your answers.
   - Was I adequately prepared for today's session?
   - Did I begin and end session 4 on time? If not, how can I help make sure our time is used more wisely in session 5?
   - Does anyone need extra encouragement this week? Follow up with a card or a phone call, if appropriate.
   - What was my overall impression of session 4?
3. Read "Before the Session" on page 19 to learn what preparations you need to make for session 5.

PLAN B

BEFORE THE SESSION

1. Prepare an overview of Acts 4:13—7:60, highlighting events described in those chapters.

2. Write the following quotation on poster board or on a tear sheet and hang it on the wall: "Saints … die to the world only to rise to a more intense life."[1]

3. If you have access to the Internet, visit the Web site *www.voiceofthemartyrs.org* to learn the story of a Christian group that is being persecuted today. Prepare to read or summarize the account during the session.

4. Have available an index card for each member. Provide tear sheets and markers for group activities.

Child Care Open, Attendance and Homework Check (15 mins.)

DURING THE SESSION

Group Session—Welcome, Prayer, and Discussion (50 mins.)

1. Have praise music playing as members arrive.

2. Ask group members to form pairs and share prayer requests. Allow time for them to pray. Encourage them to continue praying for one another throughout the week.

3. Share the overview of Acts 4:13—7:60.

4. Ask a volunteer to read Acts 8:1-4. Discuss as a group how verse 4 could change the way you pray about the persecution of Christians today.

5. Read Hebrews 13:3. Read the story of the Christian group that is being persecuted today, if you found this information. Pause and pray for these and other believers who are being persecuted, as well as for their persecutors.

6. Form small groups of from three to five persons each. Give each group a tear sheet and ask groups to list as many prejudices as possible in three minutes. Then ask groups to share their lists with the entire group and hang them on the wall.

7. Discuss the question on page 75: "Why is it so much easier to hate from a distance?"

8. Give each group member an index card. Ask members to write down their prejudices. Assure them that no one else will read them. This is between the individual and God. Ask a volunteer to read Acts 8:15. Spend time in individual prayer confessing those prejudices to God, asking for forgiveness, and praying for those they are prejudiced toward. Once you have given adequate time for individual prayer, close the prayer time by thanking God for our salvation through Christ and the forgiveness of sin. After the prayer time, place a trash basket in the middle of the room and ask members to tear up their cards and throw them away. Read Psalm 103:12 as a reminder that God not only forgives our sin but also forgets.

9. Ask for personal testimonies in response to the question on page 76: "How has God dramatically changed your attitude toward some target of your personal prejudice?"

10. Divide members into small groups. Give each group a tear sheet and a marker. Ask groups to list ways to extend the hand of fellowship to people. Then have them share with the large group.

11. Ask and discuss: Why are we sometimes so reluctant to extend the hand of fellowship? Discuss the statement on the poster: "Saints … die to the world only to rise to a more intense life."

12. Remain in small groups to discuss answers to the question on page 88, "What is the difference [between the call to the world and the call of the world]?"

Break and Return to Group (10 mins.)

View Video Segment 4 (50 mins.)

Closing Assignment and Prayer (5 mins.)

13. Ask members to complete their daily assignments in week 5 before the next group session.

14. Close by asking those who were willing to admit on page 91 that they are desperate for a surplus of love and acceptance to raise their hands. Surround these members and pray over them. Read Isaiah 54:10 and Psalm 90:14. Ask God to remind all of you of His love toward you.

---

[1]Lynn M. Poland, "The New Criticism, Neoorthodoxy, and the New Testament," as quoted in R. Alan Culpepper, *John, the Son of Zebedee: The Life of a Legend* (Minneapolis: First Fortress Press, 2000), 139.

VIDEO RESPONSE SHEET
Group Session 4

Part 1: Grasping the Concept of Divinely Inspired Scripture

According to 2 Timothy 3:16, "All Scripture is __God__ - __breathed__." The original Greek word is *theopneustos. Theo*—*God. Pneustos*—*breath* or *spirit.* Consider each of the following Scriptures.

1. Based on a comparison between 2 Peter 1:20-21 and 1 Chronicles 28:19, we might say the men God used to write Scripture served as neither the __author__ nor the __ink__. They served as the __quill__. The author is God the Holy Spirit and the ink flowing through that pen is the Holy Spirit, the breath of God that He's pouring through.

2. The Word is __eternal__, but God chose to give inspiration through __progressive__ __revelation__ (see Ps. 119:89).

3. Compare Genesis 2:7. When God breathes, He breathes __life__. Hebrews 4:12 tells us His Word is __alive__.

4. See Luke 1:1-3. We are told that __many__ undertook writing accounts of Christ's life and fulfillment of God's plan; yet we don't have "many" of those accounts in the Bible.

Part 2: Grasping God's Primary Intention Through His Inspiration of John's Gospel
Read John 1:1.

1. One of the overriding themes in the Gospel of John is presented from the very first verse: Under the inspiration of the Holy Spirit, John wanted his reader to know and recognize the __Word__.

2. The Greek term for *Word* is __Logos__. Basically it refers to the __expression__ of God __revealed__ to man. God revealed Himself through His __Son__ and His __words__.

3. The only way we will ever really know the Word, both the Person and the print, is to know His __words__. Both of these verses employ the Greek word __rhema__.

4. As we learn to receive and apply *rhema*, we are wise to remember that God's Word is written:
__by__ God about __God__, __to__ others about __others__, __to__ us about __us__.

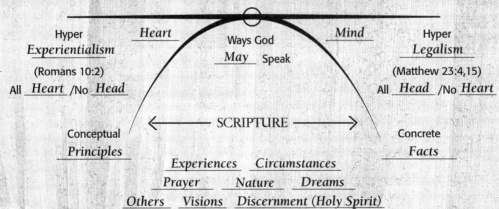

FUNDAMENTAL __Truths__
VALID __Experiences__

PROVERBS 23:7 (KJV)

	Heart	Ways God May Speak	Mind	
Hyper *Experientialism* (Romans 10:2)				Hyper *Legalism* (Matthew 23:4,15)
All __Heart__/No __Head__				All __Head__/No __Heart__

← SCRIPTURE →

Conceptual __Principles__   Concrete __Facts__

__Experiences__   __Circumstances__
__Prayer__   __Nature__   __Dreams__
__Others__   __Visions__   __Discernment__ (Holy Spirit)

Receiving His Fullness

SESSION 5

PLAN A

BEFORE THE SESSION

Refer to page 19 for a list of preparatory actions.

Child Care Open, Attendance and Homework Check (15 mins.)

DURING THE SESSION

Large Group—Welcome, Worship, and Prayer (15 mins.)
1. Greet members and hand out name tags.
2. Lead a time of worship and praise.
3. Pray, asking for God's presence and blessing.
4. Dismiss to small groups.

Small Groups (45 mins.)
1. Ask for prayer requests and have prayer (5 mins.).
2. Review the week's Principle Questions and Personal Discussion Questions (40 mins.).

Day 1
- *Principle Question:* How does Hebrews 11:6 echo the idea of godly hedonism?
- *Personal Discussion:* Write in your own words what you think Piper's statement means: "God is most glorified in us when we are most satisfied in Him."[1]

Day 2
- *Principle Question:* According to John 20:30-31, what was John's purpose in the Gospel of John?
- *Personal Discussion:* If your life were a Gospel like John's, who could people believe your Jesus to be? Respond specifically and concretely.

Day 3
- *Principle Question:* What was the obvious and eternal significance of the wedding in Cana in John 2?
- *Personal Discussion:* When was the last time you attended a party centered on Christ's presence? Briefly describe it.

Day 4
- *Principle Question:* What does Psalm 147:4 tell us about the estimated one hundred billion stars in our galaxy alone?

- *Personal Discussion:* What did David seem to be feeling when he wrote Psalm 8:3-4?

Day 5
- *Principle Question:* What happened to the soldiers after Christ responded, " 'I am He' " in John 18:6?
- *Personal Discussion:* What do the "I am" statements mean to you?

If time allows, ask for ways God spoke in week 5.

Conclude the 40-minute discussion time by thanking and affirming members. If you are using the video, do so now. If not, dismiss with a few introductory words about week 6 and a closing prayer.

Break and Return to Large Group (5 mins.)

View Video Presentation 5 (50 mins.)

Closing Assignment and Prayer (5 mins.)
1. Give a brief response to the video.
2. Briefly introduce week 6 and encourage members to complete the study before the next session.
3. Close with prayer and collect name tags.

AFTER THE SESSION
1. Immediately record concerns or impressions you had to pray for members. Pray for these throughout the week.
2. Evaluate session 5 by asking yourself the following questions and recording your answers:
   - Was I adequately prepared for today's session?
   - Did I begin and end session 5 on time? If not, how can I help make sure our time is used more wisely in session 6?
   - Does anyone need extra encouragement this week? Follow up with a card or a phone call, if appropriate.
   - What was my overall impression of session 5?
3. Read "Before the Session" on page 19 to learn what preparations you need to make for session 6.

---

[1]John Piper, *The Dangerous Duty of Delight* (Sisters, OH: Multnomah Publishers, 2001), 21.

PLAN B

BEFORE THE SESSION

1. Write the following assignments for activity 5 on separate index cards.
   - *Group 1: Moses in Exodus 33:13,15-18*
   - *Group 2: David in Psalm 63:3-7*
   - *Group 3: Paul in Philippians 3:8-10,14*
   - *Group 4: Peter in 1 Peter 1:6-9*

2. Write the following statement on poster board or on a tear sheet and hang it on the wall: *When we're not filled with the good things Christ came to bring us, we will grasp at substitutes. An unsatisfied soul is a disaster waiting to happen.*

3. Write the seven "I am" passages from the Book of John on sentence strips and hang them around the room (see activity, p. 110). Be sure to include the Scripture reference from which each "I am" statement is taken. Also hang an empty strip beside each Scripture slip.

4. Arrange to have snacks at the end of the session for a time of celebration.

5. Provide tear sheets and markers for group activities.

Child Care Open, Attendance and Homework Check (15 mins.)

DURING THE SESSION

Group Session—Welcome, Prayer, and Discussion (50 mins.)

1. Have praise music playing as group members arrive.

2. Begin by quoting John 3:16 together and pray, thanking God for the gift of His one and only Son.

3. Based on John 1:14-16 and the definition of *grace* on page 94, ask volunteers to share the phrase that means the most to them and why.

4. Read C. S. Lewis' statement on page 95. Have group members share what they think Lewis meant by the statement "We are far too easily pleased."[1]

5. Divide into four small groups and give each group one of the index cards you prepared with assignments. Ask each group to read its assigned passage and to describe the personal gain that came to these men in their pursuits of God.

6. Ask, What are some sources from outside the Bible from which many of us derive our impressions and definitions of Jesus? Compile a list on a marker board or on a tear sheet on the wall.

7. Ask volunteers to share anything they have witnessed that they would consider to be an unquestionable miracle of God.

8. Divide into triads. Read the statement on the poster (see step 2, "Before the Session"). Then ask: Have you discovered this precept to be accurate? If so, how? List on a marker board or on a tear sheet substitutes that people use to fill an unsatisfied soul.

9. Do the activity on pages 106–7 as a group. Assign verses to group members and ask them to read them aloud. Finally, ask, What are some of the basic themes of these passages?

10. Write the number 100 billion on a marker board or on a tear sheet on the wall. Point out to the group that an estimated one hundred billion stars are in our galaxy alone. Read Psalm 147:4. Ask members to share what it means to them to know that the God who created the world also created human beings. Ask, What does John 3:16 mean to you?

11. Draw attention to the "I am" statements on strips around the room. Ask each group member to stand beside the "I am" statement that means the most to her today. Have members share why that particular statement means the most to them.

12. Ask members to look up the references that accompany their statements and to write on the blank strips beside the passage how the title is associated with us.

Break and Return to Group (10 mins.)

View Video Segment 5 (50 mins.)

Closing Assignment and Prayer (5 mins.)

13. Ask members to complete their daily assignments in week 6 before the next group session.

14. End the study time by praising God as the great I Am and His Son, Jesus, as the fulfillment of every need we can have. Thank Him for His all-sufficient grace.

15. Close with a time of celebration. You are halfway through the study. Congratulations! Keep up the good work. Enjoy snacks together and fellowship. Celebrate the truths you have learned by sharing testimonies, giving all praise to God.

---

[1]C. S. Lewis, *The Weight of Glory* (Grand Rapids: Eerdmans, 1965), 1–2, as quoted in John Piper, *The Dangerous Duty of Delight* (Sisters, OH: Multnomah Publishers, 2001), 22.

VIDEO RESPONSE SHEET

Group Session 5

See John 3:5. One of the most often repeated phrases from the mouth of Christ is " _I_ _tell_ _you_ _the_ _truth_ ." In the NIV the phrase appears _77_ times in the Gospels.

Jesus used the phrase …

1. For the sake of _____ _emphasis_ _____ .

2. For clarity on issues of _____ _profound_ _____ _importance_ _____ like _life_ and _death_ .

3. For clarity on issues of _____ _controversy_ _____ .

   Christ tells us the truth. _Truth_ _breeds_ _trust_ .

Take a good look at Psalm 31:1-5,13-16,21. Camp on the words in verse 14: "I trust in you, O Lord." What makes a person able to trust God when the circumstances around him are screaming to disbelieve? He has come to trust in the God of truth (v. 5).

1. Christ will tell us the truth even when we think we'd prefer a lie. Why?

   • Because He _is_ _Truth_ (John 14:6).

   • Because only the truth _sets_ _us_ _free_ (John 8:32).

2. Thankfully, Christ's truth always comes coupled with His _____ _grace_ _____ .

3. Christ holds His _____ _church_ _____ and His _____ _children_ _____ responsible for telling not only

   His truth but His _____ _whole_ _____ truth.

Two extremes in unbalanced teaching or portraying:

God has nothing to do with anything we could ever _____ _interpret_ _____ as _____ _negative_ _____ or _____ _painful_ _____ (2 Tim. 4:3-5).

God is always _____ _angry_ _____ , never _____ _pleased_ _____ , and usually _out_ to _get_ _us_ (Luke 4:18).

See John 16:33. Christ Jesus came to us as the exact representation of the Father. He taught neither of the above extremes. See Matthew 18:4-7.

Life More Abundantly

SESSION 6

PLAN A

BEFORE THE SESSION
Refer to page 19 for a list of preparatory actions.

Child Care Open, Attendance and Homework Check (15 mins.)

DURING THE SESSION
Large Group—Welcome, Worship, and Prayer (15 mins.)
1. Greet members and hand out name tags.
2. Lead a time of worship and praise.
3. Pray, asking for God's presence and blessing.
4. Dismiss to small groups.

Small Groups (45 mins.)
1. Ask for prayer requests and have prayer (5 mins.).
2. Review the week's Principle Questions and Personal Discussion Questions (40 mins.).

Day 1
- *Principle Question:* According to 1 Corinthians 2:9-14, why is the Holy Spirit so vital in a relationship with God through His Word?
- *Personal Discussion:* What do you need most from the Holy Spirit?

Day 2
- *Principle Question:* In what ways does Christ love His own (see John 15:9)?
- *Personal Discussion:* What kinds of things hold us back from immensely productive lives?

Day 3
- *Principle Question:* Based on context and Christ's response to Judas' question in John 14:19-25, what did Christ mean when He said that soon the world would not see Him but His disciples would see Him?
- *Personal Discussion:* Are you more like a porcupine or a puppy in terms of receiving the demonstrative love of God (whether through His Word, through His Spirit bearing witness in your inner being, or through a human vessel)?

Day 4
- *Principle Question:* What were some of the encounters Jesus had with women in Scripture?
- *Personal Discussion:* To which of the women in today's reading do you most relate? Why?

Day 5
- *Principle Question:* What was the ultimate reason Jesus exercised restraint over His divine rights in Matthew 26:53-54?
- *Personal Discussion:* What are a few things you would like to have called "mine," but life experiences proved otherwise?

If time allows, ask for ways God spoke in week 6.

Conclude the 40-minute discussion time by thanking and affirming members. If you are using the video, do so now. If not, dismiss with a few introductory words about week 7 and a closing prayer.

Break and Return to Large Group (5 mins.)

View Video Presentation 6 (50 mins.)

Closing Assignment and Prayer (5 mins.)
1. Give a brief response to the video.
2. Briefly introduce week 7 and encourage members to complete the study before the next session.
3. Close with prayer and collect name tags.

AFTER THE SESSION
1. Immediately record concerns or impressions you had to pray for members. Pray for these throughout the week.
2. Evaluate session 6 by asking yourself the following questions and recording your answers.
   - Was I adequately prepared for today's session?
   - Did I begin and end session 6 on time? If not, how can I help make sure our time is used more wisely in session 7?
   - Does anyone need extra encouragement this week? Follow up with a card or a phone call, if appropriate.
   - What was my overall impression of session 6?
3. Read "Before the Session" on page 19 to learn what preparations you need to make for session 7.

PLAN B

BEFORE THE SESSION

1. Write the following statement on neon-colored poster board and place at the front of the room: *The Holy Spirit is the key to everything in a believer's life.*
2. Prepare three assignment sheets with the following instructions.
   - *Read John 15:1-17 and list everything you can about Christ's Father.*
   - *Read John 15:1-17 and list everything you can about Christ.*
   - *Read John 15:1-17 and list everything you can about Christ's disciples.*
3. Provide crayons, markers, and sheets of paper for activity 6.
4. Provide blank sheets of paper for the closing activity.
5. Provide tear sheets and markers for group activities.

Child Care Open, Attendance and Homework Check (15 mins.)

DURING THE SESSION

Group Session—Welcome, Prayer, and Discussion (50 mins.)

1. Open the session by sharing testimonies of ways God has shown Himself this past week. Spend time praising Him.
2. Discuss as a group the question on page 116, "What difference could the Spirit of God make when living *in* a person, as opposed to *with* a person?" Call attention to the neon poster and discuss the statement "The Holy Spirit is the key to everything in a believer's life."
3. As a group, make a list of wrong motives we might use in making requests to God. Record these on a marker board or on a tear sheet on the wall.
4. Divide members into three groups and give them the assignment sheets you prepared. Allow time for group work; then call for reports.
5. Ask members to form pairs. Say: Based on John 15:1-17, God offers both a love we can live in and a source we can draw from. Share with your partner which of those offers you have personally experienced and which offer you need to trust more.
6. Distribute crayons, markers, and sheets of paper. Ask group members to draw their favorite places where they have seen God reveal His glory. Remind the group that this activity is not to discover the best artists but to give members an opportunity to remember special times when God has revealed His glory through nature. If some want to show their works of art, let them, but don't force anyone to share.
7. Divide into groups of four and ask each group to list on tear sheets ways Christ discloses Himself to us other than those on pages 126–27.
8. Divide members into six groups and assign each group a passage of Scripture from the assignment on pages 128–30. Have each group discuss the questions related to its passage of Scripture. Ask each group to write a modern-day example of that Scripture or to paraphrase the verses and share how Jesus longs to meet the need. After groups have had time to complete their work, call for reports.
9. As a group, list as many of the concepts John either presented *more* or with greater emphasis in his Gospel. Instruct members to do this activity from memory. No cheating!
10. Assign the verses on page 133 to group members. Ask them to read the verses aloud and to describe how each underscores identification by association.

Break and Return to Group (10 mins.)

View Video Segment 6 (50 mins.)

Closing Assignment and Prayer (5 mins.)
11. Ask members to complete their daily assignments in week 7 before the next group session.
12. Distribute blank sheets of paper. Close by asking group members to write prayers expressing thanksgiving to God for the right of sonship.

VIDEO RESPONSE SHEET

Group Session 6

Our previous lesson concluded the written focus on the concepts of "more" and "abundance" in the Gospel of John. Today we will pick up and expand on an important principle for the believers life that

was established in week 6, day 5: _____*identification*_____ _*by*_ _____*association*_____. No other chapter in all four Gospels has "more" to say about this wonderful principle than the incomparable John 17.

In contrast, man's natural life principle is: _____*identification*_____ _*by*_ _____*exaltation*_____.

"Identification by association" is beautifully illustrated in John 17.

1. Between _____*Father*_____ and _*Son*_. Read John 17:1-5.
   A. Traces of Intimacy

   - In _____*timing*_____ (the time has come ...)

   - In the essence of _____*eternal*_____ _____*life*_____

   - In reference to relationship _____*before*_____ the _____*world*_____ began

   B. Terms of Intercession

   - "_____*Glorify*_____ your _____*Son*_____, that your Son may _____*glorify*_____ _____*you*_____."

   - Identification by association for _____*glorification*_____.

2. Between Father, Son, and _____*those*_____ God _____*gave*_____ _____*Him*_____. Read John 17:6,20.
   A. Traces of Intimacy
   - The revelation of the Father received through ...

     1) Obedience to His _____*Word*_____ (logos)

     2) Acceptance of His _____*words*_____ (rhema)

   - Christ's insistence that _____*glory*_____ had come to Him through them

   - Christ's passion for the _____*love*_____ God has for Him

   B. Terms of Intercession

   - "protect them by the _____*power*_____ of your _____*name*_____"

   - "protect them from the _____*evil*_____ _____*one*_____"

   - "that all of them may be _____*one*_____ ... brought to _____*complete*_____ _____*unity*_____"

Letters from the Heart

SESSION 7

PLAN A

BEFORE THE SESSION

Refer to page 19 for a list of preparatory actions.

Child Care Open, Attendance and Homework Check (15 mins.)

DURING THE SESSION

Large Group—Welcome, Worship, and Prayer (15 mins.)
1. Greet members and hand out name tags.
2. Lead a time of worship and praise.
3. Pray, asking for God's presence and blessing.
4. Dismiss to small groups.

Small Groups (45 mins.)
1. Ask for prayer requests and have prayer (5 mins.).
2. Review the week's Principle Questions and Personal Discussion Questions (40 mins.).

Day 1
• *Principle Question:* According to 1 John 1:9, what is the secret to sharing a life of fellowshipping with Christ and walking in the light?
• *Personal Discussion:* What have you experienced through your *koinonia* relationship with the Father and the Son that you almost cannot stand for others to miss?

Day 2
• *Principle Question:* How did Paul describe God's love in Ephesians 3:18-19?
• *Personal Discussion:* Deep in your heart, what are you most afraid of?

Day 3
• *Principle Question:* Why do we love, according to 1 John 4:19?
• *Personal Discussion:* Have you found this principle to be true (that loving difficult people is important to God, so He continually brings these relationships into our lives)? ❑ Yes ❑ No If so, estimate how many persons you've been very challenged to love in the past five years. _____ If any of those relationships became some of your dearest, please explain.

Day 4
• *Principle Question:* What do John's words "love in truth" in 2 John mean?
• *Personal Discussion:* What do you tend to focus on during a microscope day?

Day 5
• *Principle Question:* How did Paul describe the participation of labor between a believer and God in Colossians 1:29?
• *Personal Discussion:* Write what you think a one-sentence description of your life would say. Then describe what you would want it to say.

If time allows, ask for ways God spoke in week 7.

Conclude the 40-minute discussion time by thanking and affirming members. If you are using the video, do so now. If not, dismiss with a few introductory words about week 8 and a closing prayer.

Break and Return to Large Group (5 mins.)

View Video Presentation 7 (50 mins.)

Closing Assignment and Prayer (5 mins.)
1. Give a brief response to the video.
2. Briefly introduce week 8 and encourage members to complete the study before the next session.
3. Close with prayer and collect name tags.

AFTER THE SESSION
1. Immediately record concerns or impressions you had to pray for members. Pray for these throughout the week.
2. Evaluate session 7 by asking yourself the following questions and recording your answers.
   • Was I adequately prepared for today's session?
   • Did I begin and end session 7 on time? If not, how can I help make sure our time is used more wisely in session 8?
   • Does anyone need extra encouragement this week? Follow up with a card or a phone call, if appropriate.
   • What was my overall impression of session 7?
3. Read "Before the Session" on page 19 to learn what preparations you need to make for session 8.

PLAN B

BEFORE THE SESSION

1. Make a copy of the responsive reading below, based on 1 John 1:5-10; 2:1-2, for each member.
2. Prepare the following assignment sheets for activity 4.
   - Group 1: 1 John 3:1-3
   - Group 2: 1 John 3:19-22
   - Group 3: 1 John 4:13-18
3. Prepare the following assignment sheets for activity 6.
   - Group 1: 1 John 3:11-15
   - Group 2: 1 John 3:16-22
   - Group 3: 1 John 4:7-12
   - Group 4: 1 John 4:16-21
   - Group 5: 1 John 5:1-5
4. Provide tear sheets and markers for group activities.

Child Care Open, Attendance and Homework Check (15 mins.)

DURING THE SESSION
Group Session—Welcome, Prayer, and Discussion (50 mins.)

1. Hand out and read the responsive reading.
2. Ask members to turn to and read silently 1 John 1:4 and John 15:11. Ask, Do you see similarities between the catalysts for complete joy? Encourage sharing.
3. Ask members to share their responses to the question on page 139, "What have you experienced through your *koinonia* relationship with the Father and the Son that you almost cannot stand for others to miss?"
4. Divide members into three groups and give each group one of the assignment sheets you prepared. Ask groups to read their assigned verses and to record everything we can know and apply about God's love for us.
5. Ask members to share their answers to the first two activities on page 143. Ask them to describe how they imagine the property with a condemned house on it looks. Ask, What might your sign have said?

6. Divide members into five groups and give each group one of the assignment sheets you prepared. Each group is to read the verses and determine what the passage says about love. Then the group should determine a creative way to present its findings with the group. Some ideas are drama, art, and music.
7. As a group, share responses to the activity on page 147: "Glance over the entire letter of 1 John. How often do you find terms of endearment for his readers, and what are they?" List these on a marker board or on a tear sheet.
8. Ask members to name lies Satan confronts us with. List these on a marker board or on a tear sheet on the wall.
9. Divide members into three groups and name each group Gaius, Diotrephes, or Demetrius. Ask each group to read about the assigned man in 3 John and to write an epitaph for him. Give groups tear sheets to record their completed epitaphs.
10. Ask group members to give examples of Sabbath moments (see pp. 155–56).

Break and Return to Group (10 mins.)

View Video Segment 7 (50 mins.)

Closing Assignment and Prayer (5 mins.)

11. Ask members to complete their daily assignments in week 8 before the next group session.
12. Challenge members over the next week to take time for rest. Assign each member a partner and have partners exchange phone numbers. Encourage partners to call each other for accountability.
13. Close by thanking God for our fellowship with the Father, Son, and Holy Spirit. Thank Him for His amazing love and for the love letters He sent us through John. Pray that we might love as He loves us.

WALKING IN THE LIGHT

Leader: God is light, and in Him is no darkness at all.

Group: If we say that we have fellowship with Him, and walk in darkness, we lie, and do not practice the truth:

Leader: But if we walk in the light, as He is in the light, we have fellowship with one with another, and the blood of Jesus Christ His Son cleanses us from all sin.

Group: If we say that we have no sin, we deceive ourselves, and the truth is not in us.

Leader: If we confess our sins, he is faithful and just to forgive us our sins, and to cleanse us from all unrighteousness.

Group: If we say that we have not sinned, we make Him a liar, and His word is not in us.

Leader: If any man sin, we have an advocate with the Father, Jesus Christ the righteous:

Group: And He is the propitiation for our sins: and not for ours only, but also for the sins of the whole world.

VIDEO RESPONSE SHEET
Group Session 7

Our journey with the apostle John will take us now over the waters of the Aegean Sea to a small island called Patmos. In week 8, day 1 we will look more closely at John's arrival and the introduction to the Book of Revelation. Today, however, we're going to consider to the best of our understanding the vision of Christ that John recorded in **Revelation 1:9-18.**

While we understand that John received a one-time-only vision of Christ, I believe we can draw some important parallels about becoming the kind of people to whom Christ can reveal Himself.

1. Though a prisoner in exile, John remained spiritually ___*keen*___ and ___*fervent*___.

   Revelation 1:10, "On the ___*Lord's*___ ___*Day*___ I was in ___*the*___ ___*Spirit*___."

2. John was faithful with what he "___*heard*___," and God invited him to "___*see*___" (Rev 1:10,12).

   The original word for *hear* often used in Scripture is *akouo,* meaning "not only to hear but to

   ___*respond*___ and ___*obey*___."

3. John came to the startling realization that the immortal Christ ___*exceeded*___

   ___*anything*___ he could have ___*stretched*___ his ___*mind*___ to imagine (v. 17).

4. John encountered the ___*tender*___ ___*familiarity*___ wrapped in the complete

   unfamiliarity of ___*unveiled*___ "___*God*___-___*ness*___" (v. 17).

5. Conspicuously ___*absent*___ in the record of John's staggering encounter with the

   immortal Christ is a ___*single*___ ___*word*___ from the ___*disciple's*___ ___*mouth*___ (Eccl. 5:1-2).

Among the Lampstands

SESSION 8

PLAN A

BEFORE THE SESSION

Refer to page 19 for a list of preparatory actions.

Child Care Open, Attendance and Homework Check (15 mins.)

DURING THE SESSION

Large Group—Welcome, Worship, and Prayer (15 mins.)
1. Greet members and hand out name tags.
2. Lead a time of worship and praise.
3. Pray, asking for God's presence and blessing.
4. Dismiss to small groups.

Small Groups (45 mins.)
1. Ask for prayer requests and have prayer (5 mins.).
2. Review the week's Principle Questions and Personal Discussion Questions (40 mins.).

Day 1
- *Principle Question:* What does Jeremiah 32:17 say about God?
- *Personal Discussion:* What kinds of clouds—if any—are in your life?

Day 2
- *Principle Question:* What does Christ pinpoint about Himself to the church in Ephesus in Revelation 2:1? What is the corresponding verse in the Revelation 1 vision?
- *Personal Discussion:* How does the command to return to your first love speak to you?

Day 3
- *Principle Question:* According to 1 Peter 1:6-9, how are believers able to be faithful in suffering?
- *Personal Discussion:* Do you know a believer in Christ whose faithfulness astounds you in the midst of his or her suffering? If so, describe him or her.

Day 4
- *Principle Question:* Based on Hosea 11:3-4, what does God say about healing?
- *Personal Discussion:* How have you personally seen the enemy counterfeit one of God's benefits?

Day 5
- *Principle Question:* What was the promise, and to whom would it come (see Rev. 2:26-28)?
- *Personal Discussion:* What are some ways that we women can misuse our sexuality?

If time allows, ask for ways God spoke in week 8.

Conclude the 40-minute discussion time by thanking and affirming members. If you are using the video, do so now. If not, dismiss with a few introductory words about week 9 and a closing prayer.

Break and Return to Large Group (5 mins.)

View Video Presentation 8 (50 mins.)

Closing Assignment and Prayer (5 mins.)
1. Give a brief response to the video.
2. Briefly introduce week 9 and encourage members to complete the study before the next session.
3. Close with prayer and collect name tags.

AFTER THE SESSION
1. Immediately record concerns or impressions you had to pray for members. Pray for these throughout the week.
2. Evaluate session 8 by asking yourself the following questions and recording your answers.
   - Was I adequately prepared for today's session?
   - Did I begin and end session 8 on time? If not, how can I help make sure our time is used more wisely in session 9?
   - Does anyone need extra encouragement this week? Follow up with a card or a phone call, if appropriate.
   - What was my overall impression of session 8?
3. Read "Before the Session" on page 19 to learn what preparations you need to make for session 9.

PLAN B

BEFORE THE SESSION

1. Make the following assignment sheets for activity 4.

Group 1—Ephesus
Read Revelation 2:1-7.
- *List pertinent information from page 164.*
- *What warning did Christ give the church in verse 5?*
- *What was Christ's message to the overcomers in the church in Ephesus?*
- *What lessons can the church today learn from Christ's message to the church in Ephesus?*

Group 2—Smyrna
Read Revelation 2:8-11.
- *List pertinent information from pages 166–67.*
- *What are some facts about Smyrna?*
- *What was missing in Christ's message to the church in Smyrna?*
- *What lessons can the church today learn from Christ's message to the church in Smyrna?*

Group 3—Pergamum
Read Revelation 2:12-17.
- *List pertinent information from pages 170-71.*
- *What are some facts about Pergamum?*
- *What two things did Christ promise to those who overcame?*
- *What lessons can the church today learn from Christ's message to the church in Pergamum?*

Group 4—Thyatira
Read Revelation 2:18-29.
- *List pertinent information from page 174.*
- *What was Thyatira known for? What are some other facts about Thyatira?*
- *Who are the two women Scripture associates with Thyatira? Describe both women.*
- *What lessons can the church today learn from Christ's message to the church in Thyatira?*

2. Provide tear sheets and markers for group activities.

Child Care Open, Attendance and Homework Check (15 mins.)

DURING THE SESSION

Group Session—Welcome, Prayer, and Discussion (50 mins.)

1. Open with a time of praise. Ask members to speak aloud the titles and descriptions of Jesus in Revelation 1:4-8. Use this praise time to focus everyone's attention on Jesus.
2. Have members discuss the question on page 159: "What do you think John meant by the reasons he gave for being on Patmos?"
3. Ask, What are the repeated components in Jesus' message to the churches? List responses on a marker board or on a tear sheet on the wall.
4. Divide into four groups and give each group one of the assignment sheets you prepared. Also give each group a tear sheet and a marker. Give groups as much time as possible to work, leaving adequate time for reports.
5. Call for group reports. Allow the entire group to share insights or ask questions.

Break and Return to Group (10 mins.)

View Video Segment 8 (50 mins.)

Closing Assignment and Prayer (5 mins.)

6. Ask members to complete their daily assignments in week 9 before the next group session.
7. Allow a few moments for members to reflect on the video presentation and on week 8 and to jot down one major truth God impressed on them. Close by giving an opportunity for members to thank God for this truth and to help them apply it in their lives. Close the prayer time by asking God to give these women wisdom and grace to be overcomers and to receive all that Christ has waiting for them.

Group Session 8

In the midst of many symbols and shrouds, the Book of Revelation frames several visions of such startling clarity and detail that we could stand before them for hours and continue to discover something new. **Revelation 7:9-17** encases one of those.

As we study these Scriptures, let your imagination play like a videotape. We'll push the pause button on several different elements in the scene and see what we can glean.

1. A great _____ **multitude** _____ that can't be counted standing before the _____ **throne** _____

   and in front of the _____ **Lamb** _____

   This multitude is …

   • Every _____ **nation** _____: *ethnos*—set apart by location, customs, and laws

   • Every _____ **tribe** _____: *phule*—set apart by blood lines tracing to common ancestors

   • Every _____ **people** _____: *laos*—set apart by various common bonds of a society

   • Every _____ **language** _____: *glossa*—set apart by dialects or languages

   These four descriptions represent every means of division between the inhabitants of earth.

2. Those who have come out of (the) _____ **great** _____ **tribulation** _____ (v. 14).
   Carefully note that scholars are divided about the exact meaning of this phrase. Some believe the masses of people pictured have come out of "great tribulation" (as may be implied in the KJV and could simply imply Acts 14:22), while others believe they have come out of "*the* great tribulation" (as *may* be implied in the NIV and NASB). *If* Scripture means *the* great tribulation, this gathering suggests that the most profound evangelical movement in church history will occur during the most dreadful days of human history.

Compare Revelation 6:9-11. Many scholars believe these martyrs are among those gathered in Revelation 7:9.

3. The consummation of _____ **perfect** _____ **unity** _____ in glorious _____ **diversity** _____. Please don't

   miss the fact that these "nations, tribes, and peoples" are gathered as one, but—at least in this vision

   and for this time—retain some level of distinction.

4. The _____ **worship** _____ of the _____ **angels** _____ (vv. 11-12). "Amen!"

5. The _____ **tent** _____ of God (vv. 15-17)

From a Throne's Eye View

SESSION 9

PLAN A

BEFORE THE SESSION

Refer to page 19 for a list of preparatory actions.

Child Care Open, Attendance and Homework Check (15 mins.)

DURING THE SESSION

Large Group—Welcome, Worship, and Prayer (15 mins.)
1. Greet members and hand out name tags.
2. Lead a time of worship and praise.
3. Pray, asking for God's presence and blessing.
4. Dismiss to small groups.

Small Groups (45 mins.)
1. Ask for prayer requests and have prayer (5 mins.).
2. Review the week's Principle Questions and Personal Discussion Questions (40 mins.).

Day 1
- *Principle Question:* How could a chronic fear of death inhibit a believer's entire life and ministry? What does Hebrews 2:14 say about the subject?
- *Personal Discussion:* Have you ever seen yourself or someone you love interpret rejection as a deathblow? ❑ Yes ❑ No If so, explain.

Day 2
- *Principle Question:* For what did Christ commend the church in Philadelphia after acknowledging its "little strength" in Revelation 3:8?
- *Personal Discussion:* Why do you think the need to matter is sacred?

Day 3
- *Principle Question:* How did the church at Laodicea describe itself (see Rev. 3:17)?
- *Personal Discussion:* How do you most make yourself useful?

Day 4
- *Principle Question:* Where is the Lamb depicted as standing in Revelation 5:6?
- *Personal Discussion:* List three of your greatest challenges or concerns.

Day 5
- *Principle Question:* How did John respond when no one was found to open the scroll in Revelation 5:4?
- *Personal Discussion:* How do you feel about the fact that the plan of redemption was obviously already set in motion before humans were created?

If time allows, ask for ways God spoke in week 9.

Conclude the 40-minute discussion time by thanking and affirming members. If you are using the video, do so now. If not, dismiss with a few introductory words about week 10 and a closing prayer.

Break and Return to Large Group (5 mins.)

View Video Presentation 9 (50 mins.)

Closing Assignment and Prayer (5 mins.)
1. Give a brief response to the video.
2. Briefly introduce week 10 and encourage members to complete the study before the next session.
3. Close with prayer and collect name tags.

AFTER THE SESSION

1. Immediately record concerns or impressions you had to pray for members. Pray for these throughout the week.
2. Evaluate session 9 by asking yourself the following questions and recording your answers.
   - Was I adequately prepared for today's session?
   - Did I begin and end session 9 on time? If not, how can I help make sure our time is used more wisely in session 10?
   - Does anyone need extra encouragement this week? Follow up with a card or a phone call, if appropriate.
   - What was my overall impression of session 9?
3. Read "Before the Session" on page 19 to learn what preparations you need to make for session 10.

PLAN B

BEFORE THE SESSION

1. Prepare the following assignment sheets.

Group 1—Sardis
Read Revelation 3:1-6.
- *List pertinent information from page 181.*
- *What are some facts about Sardis?*
- *How did the history of Sardis contribute to deadness in the church?*
- *What lessons can the church today learn from Christ's message to the church in Sardis?*

Group 2—Philadelphia
Read Revelation 3:7-13.
- *List pertinent information from page 184.*
- *What are some facts about Philadelphia?*
- *What are some pointers for ministry from the church in Philadelphia?*
- *What lessons can the church today learn from Christ's message to the church in Philadelphia?*

Group 3—Laodicea
Read Revelation 3:14-22.
- *List pertinent information from pages 188–89.*
- *What are some facts about Laodicea?*
- *What were some characteristics of the church in Laodicea?*
- *What lessons can the church today learn from Christ's message to the church in Laodicea?*

2. Be prepared to lead the group in singing "Holy, Holy, Holy." Supply hymnals or record the words on poster board or on a tear sheet.

3. *Optional:* Find a recording of "Name Above Every Name" to play as a conclusion to the session.

4. Provide tear sheets and markers for group activities.

Child Care Open, Attendance and Homework Check (15 mins.)

DURING THE SESSION

Group Session—Welcome, Prayer, and Discussion (50 mins.)

1. Begin with prayer.

2. Divide members into three groups. Give each group one of the assignment sheets you prepared, a tear sheet, and a marker. After group work, ask each to report to the entire group. Allow group members to contribute or ask questions.

3. Ask volunteers to read Isaiah 6:1-5; Ezekiel 1:22-28; and Revelation 4. List basic similarities to and descriptions of the throne room on a marker board or on a tear sheet.

4. Ask volunteers to answer the questions on page 195.

5. Lead the group in singing "Holy, Holy, Holy."

Break and Return to Group (10 mins.)

View Video Segment 9 (50 mins.)

Closing Assignment and Prayer (5 mins.)

6. *Optional:* Play the recording you obtained of "Name Above All Names."

7. Close by thanking God for the Lamb, who was slain from the foundation of the world for the salvation of the world. Praise Jesus because only He is worthy.

VIDEO RESPONSE SHEET

Group Session 9

Read Revelation 12:7-12. Revelation 12:9 calls the enemy of our souls by five names:

- The ___*great*___ ___*dragon*___

- That ___*ancient*___ ___*serpent*___

- The ___*devil*___

- ___*Satan*___

- ___*Accuser*___

Primary defenses against the accuser:

1. "By the ___*blood*___ of the ___*Lamb*___." Once we are covered by the blood of the Lamb,

   Satan can do nothing to "uncover" us. So what's a devil to do? Try to make us "feel" uncovered.

2. "By the ___*word*___ of their testimony"

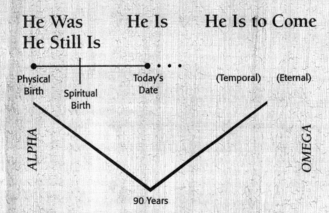

THE ACCUSER'S FORMULA

Your ___*Is*___
- Your ___*Was*___
+ Your ___*Is-to-Come*___
—————————————
Incomplete

GOD'S FORMULA

___*Redeemed*___ was
+ ___*Cleansed*___ is
—————————————
Powerful Is-to-Come

Blessed Benediction

SESSION 10

PLAN A

BEFORE THE SESSION
Refer to page 19 for a list of preparatory actions.

Child Care Open, Attendance and Homework Check (15 mins.)

DURING THE SESSION

Large Group—Welcome, Worship, and Prayer (15 mins.)
1. Greet members and hand out name tags.
2. Lead a time of worship and praise.
3. Pray, asking for God's presence and blessing.
4. Dismiss to small groups.

Small Groups (45 mins.)
1. Ask for prayer requests and have prayer (5 mins.).
2. Review the week's Principle Questions and Personal Discussion Questions (40 mins.).

Day 1
- *Principle Question:* How were the 144,000 marked, according to Revelation 14:1?
- *Personal Discussion:* How do you feel about having a seal marking you as Christ's for all the supernatural world to see?

Day 2
- *Principle Question:* Why will people refuse God (see Rom. 2:5)?
- *Personal Discussion:* What makes you shudder and know in your heart that God's wrath must come?

Day 3
- *Principle Question:* Exactly how will Christ strike down His foes (see Rev 19:15,21)?
- *Personal Discussion:* What are you anxious for God to avenge on your behalf?

Day 4
- *Principle Question:* In Revelation 21:14 what did John see on the 12 foundations of the city wall?
- *Personal Discussion:* To what part of this old order will you be happiest to bid farewell?

Day 5
- *Principle Question:* How had John lived the essence of John 15:12-17?
- *Personal Question:* List the kinds of things you imagine John thought and felt on the ride back to Ephesus.

If time allows, ask for ways God spoke in week 10.

Conclude the 40-minute discussion time by thanking members and affirming their participation over the past 10 weeks. If you are using the video, do so now. If not, dismiss with concluding remarks and prayer.

Break and Return to Large Group (5 mins.)

View Video Presentation 10 (50 mins.)

Closing Remarks and Prayer (10 mins. rather than 5 if you are doing an optional evaluation)
1. If you prepared an evaluation, distribute it at this time and allow 5 minutes to complete it.
2. Offer closing remarks about what has been learned.
3. Close with prayer.

AFTER THE SESSION
1. Evaluate the entire study by asking yourself:
   - Did members seem to grasp the principles?
   - Are there group members with no church home whom I should invite to visit church with me?
   - Should I remain in contact with any members to encourage them?
   - Would I consider taking another course of this kind?
   - Would I consider leading another course?
   - What was my overall impression of *Beloved Disciple*?
2. Verify participants' eligibility for Christian Growth Study Plan credit (see p. 224 in the member book). Sign Christian Growth Study Plan forms and submit them to the church office.

PLAN B

BEFORE THE SESSION
1. Enlist someone to lead a time of praise and worship or get a praise CD and a CD player to open the session.
2. Prepare the following assignment sheets for activity 4. *Group 1—the seals (Rev. 6:1-17; 8:1-5)*

Group 2—the trumpets (Rev. 8:6-13; 9:1-21)
Group 3—the bowls (Rev. 16)

3. Prepare the following assignment sheets for activity 5.
   Group 1—Revelation 19:11-21
   • *Read the passage and give this segment a title.*
   • *List facts gathered from these verses about Christ.*
   • *List facts about the beast.*
   Group 2—Revelation 20:1-6
   • *Read the passage and give this segment a title.*
   • *List all details about Satan.*
   Group 3—Revelation 20:7-10
   • *Read the passage and give this segment a title.*
   • *List all facts about Satan's defeat.*
   Group 4—Revelation 20:11-15
   • *Read the passage and give this segment a title.*
   • *List every detail about the great white throne.*
   • *What is the difference between the great-white-throne judgment and the judgment seat of Christ?*

4. Write the numbers 1–4 on small sheets of paper and tape them to the bottoms of chairs for activity 5.

5. Enlist four members to read Revelation 22 and to be prepared to report on (1) descriptions of the new heaven and earth, (2) John's personal responses, (3) warnings, (4) and invitations.

6. Be prepared to lead the group in singing "To God Be the Glory." Supply hymnals or record the words on poster board or on a tear sheet.

7. Provide tear sheets and markers for activities.

Child Care Open, Attendance and Homework Check (15 mins.)

DURING THE SESSION
Group Session—Welcome, Prayer, and Discussion (50 mins.)

1. Begin with a time of praise and worship led by the person you enlisted. Or have a sing-along, using a praise CD.

2. Divide into triads and assign them the activity at the top of page 204: "Read Revelation 13 and record every way the kingdom of darkness imitates works of the Godhead but with a twisted, evil intent."

3. Ask members to name a praise and worship song they at first found difficult and unfamiliar but over time came to love as a favorite. Ask, What made the song a favorite for you? Explain that no one else could learn the song of the 144,000 because only they had lived it.

4. Divide members into three groups and give them the assignment sheets you prepared. Ask each group to read the Scripture, note descriptions that stand out most, and list any coinciding wrath of the kingdom of

darkness as well as reactions of unredeemed humanity (particularly repentance or lack of it). Call for reports after groups have had time to work.

5. Divide members into four groups according to the numbers you placed under the chairs. Give groups the assignments you prepared. Allow time for group work. Then call for reports.

6. Ask a volunteer to read aloud Revelation 21. As a group, determine ways Revelation 21 contrasts with Revelation 20. List these on a marker board or on a tear sheet on the wall.

7. List on a marker board or on a tear sheet descriptions of the New Jerusalem found in Revelation 21.

8. Call on the four members enlisted to report on the following from Revelation 22: (1) descriptions of the new heaven and earth, (2) John's personal responses, (3) warnings, (4) and invitations.

Break and Return to Group (10 mins.)

View Video Segment 10 (50 mins.)

Closing Remarks and Prayer (5 mins.)

9. Thank members for their participation in and faithfulness to this study.

10. Read aloud Revelation 22:13-21. State that the group will close in prayer, responding to the invitation to come (see Rev. 22:17). Invite those who can kneel to do so; those who cannot kneel, to stand or sit. Praise God that Jesus is coming again! Ask Him to draw members into a deeper love relationship with Him and to to burden them to tell the good news to those who do not know Him.

11. End the study by singing "To God Be the Glory."

AFTER THE SESSION

1. Evaluate the entire study by asking yourself:
   • Did members seem to grasp the overall principles emphasized in this 10-week study?
   • Are there group members with no church home whom I should invite to visit church with me?
   • Should I remain in contact with any members of my group to encourage them?
   • Would I consider taking another course of this kind?
   • Would I consider leading another course of this kind?
   • What was my overall impression of *Beloved Disciple?*

2. Verify participants' eligibility for Christian Growth Study Plan credit (see p. 224 in the member book for more information). Sign Christian Growth Study Plan forms and submit them to the church office.

VIDEO RESPONSE SHEET

Group Session 10

1. The one-word call to worship probably has great significance (v. 7). The word *hallelujah* (NIV) or *alleluia* (KJV) comes from the original Hebrew *halelu*, meaning to ___**praise**___, and *Yah*, the shortened form of ___**Yahweh**___ or ___**Jehovah**___. With one exception (Ps. 135:3), *allellouia* is always found at the beginning or end of psalms, suggesting that it was a ___**standardized**___ call to praise in the ___**temple**___ ___**worship**___. This may suggest that, although every nation, tribe, and tongue will be part of this glorious wedding, the ceremony itself may be decidedly ___**Jewish**___.

In ancient Hebrew tradition …

2. The actual wedding arrangements were the responsibility of the ___**groom**___ and ___**his**___ ___**father**___. (See Judg. 14:10-11.)

3. The chief responsibility of the bride was to ___**prepare**___ ___**herself**___ (v. 7):

   • The bride prioritized ___**purity**___.

   • The bride took special baths of ___**clean**___ ___**water**___ and ___**fragrant**___ ___**oils**___.

   • The bride chose ___**fine**___ jewelry to wear on her wedding day.

4. During the ceremony, held under the ___**wedding**___ ___**canopy**___ or *huppah*, the bride traditionally ___**circled**___ the groom (Jer. 31:22).

5. ___**Seven**___ ___**blessings**___ were pronounced during the ceremony (Rev. 21:1-3,22-23).

6. Although deep repentance and personal cleansing took place in preparation, the actual wedding day was marked by great ___**gladness**___ of ___**heart**___ (Song of Songs 3:11).

   • Custom prohibited anyone from ___**mourning**___ or ___**fasting**___ on the day of the wedding (Rev. 19:7).

   • The original word for "be glad" is *agalliao*, which means "to ___**exult**___, rejoice with exuberance; often to ___**leap**___ for ___**joy**___, show one's joy by ___**leaping**___, ___**skipping**___, or ___**dancing**___, denoting ___**excessive**___ or ecstatic joy and delight."

Personalize Isaiah 62:5: "As a bridegroom rejoices over his bride, so will [my] ___**God**___ ___**rejoice**___ over [me]."